STUCK.
STRAINED.
STRESSED.

Real Stories About Shifting Your
Mindset to Overcome Challenges

Compiled by
Propelled Leadership LLC

TABLE OF CONTENTS

.

FORWARD

I started this book with a selfish motive: I wanted to find a mindset and set of tools that would enable me to jump forward in successfully starting a business. Being a new entrepreneur is hard for a risk-averse person like me. When I started contemplating the journey, I looked for strategies to shift the way I saw the risk. I gathered advice, support and tools from friends, colleagues, coaches and consultants. Everyone had a story to share, and I learned from them. In return, I wanted to share what I'd learned with others so that they could be inspired by the stories of courage, grit, inner peace and perspective.

This book offers personal stories from professionals on how they faced a challenge and found a way to move forward. This book is not a 'how-to' guide. The authors note that there are often no easy solutions or one-quick fixes. This book does not shy away from the reality that some days are harder than others. Even a solution that may work one day may not be the best fit for a different challenge the next. Instead, this book offers a sneak peek into the lives and authentic insights of many professionals with diverse experiences. Each journey highlighted in this book bears witness to the time, investment and recurring effort these professionals took to find their way to a change they wanted.

My hope is that by reading these stories, you find a shared experience or gain inspiration and encouragement as you set out on your own journey.

— Kate Kerr, Propelled Leadership LLC

ACKNOWLEDGMENTS

I want to thank and recognize the authors who contributed to this book. While writing a chapter may seem like an easy task, it takes significant time and effort. I want to express my sincere gratitude to everyone who shared their truth in this process, through thoughtful, personal, and honest stories.

CREATING BETTER SOIL FOR MINDSET SHIFTS

by Lori K. Mihalich-Levin

And all at once, a straight line of rosebushes exploded from the perfectly-groomed, weed-less soil, blooming overnight and producing gorgeous, magical flowers – with no assistance whatsoever from a gardener.

And all at once, with the sound of thunder clapping and the flash of a lightning bolt, a stroke of genius hit Moses. He held up his staff; the Red Sea parted. A tribe was led out of slavery, and the bodies, hearts, and minds of Jewish people everywhere were suddenly, instantaneously free.

No, no, no. Wait. Rewind those scenes.

Inspiration, evolution, and sea change – *pun intended* – don't happen in a flash the way Hollywood or fast-motion photography shows us; nor Instagram or Pinterest, for that matter. You can't play Charlton Heston, declare to your brain that it needs to be free, and suddenly, poof! Nothing is holding you back from wild success.

Sometimes, we think our minds will shift in a flash. Often, we think our new businesses will take off in a hot minute. Or worse, perhaps, we think that if there's no such flash, then we're failures with no hope for change whatsoever.

There's a more realistic middle ground, I'm here to argue, where inspiration comes by feeding ourselves with nutrients over time. Where curiosity can lead us to the next right thing. Where villages support us so we don't have to be struck by lightning bolts all by ourselves. Where our communities hold up mirrors to our own brains' foibles. And where we nourish our own creativity with the gift of idleness and space to grow.

DECIDE TO EXPERIMENT

When I started my business, Mindful Return, seven years ago, I was a self-described risk-averse lawyer. I was not an entrepreneur. I had never dreamed of owning a business, I didn't have an MBA, and I was terrified of selling something.

As I returned to work full-time after maternity leave with my second son, I declared that two children felt like eighty-five. I was drowning, and I couldn't find helpful resources to support my personal and professional identity transition into working parenthood. Wanting desperately to fill this gap, I sat down on my bed in front of my laptop with clammy, shaking hands, and started to write my first blog post.

Not having any grand design for what that first post might become helped me immensely. I viewed it as an experiment. "What might happen," I wondered, "if I write down my own experiences and start sharing those things that I wished existed in the world for new parents?" My anxious brain usually ran rapid with negative "what ifs," but this time, I was learning to ask "what if" with curiosity and optimism.

After roughly eighteen months of working full time while also running Mindful Return, I decided I wanted more daylight hours to work on my side hustle. Perhaps ironically, I thought going back to a law firm might afford me more flexibility than my full-time, meeting-filled in-house role. I decided to experiment with asking firms to hire me as Counsel on a sixty percent schedule.

What did they say? They said yes, which led me to further experiment with another question for these same firms: "Would you hire me as a Partner on a sixty percent schedule rather than as Counsel?" Yes again.

An experiment. A mere ask. A "what if?" from me, and a "why not?" from them. You can't possibly get what you don't ask for, I learned, so I've continued to experiment one day at a time. I've now been a Partner at my firm for almost six years, and I've reduced my firm schedule down to fifty percent to have even more time for Mindful Return. These "what ifs" were worth asking.

LET YOUR COMMUNITY WATER YOUR SOIL

It's hard to see the foibles of our own brains, isn't it? We perceive the thoughts that go through our heads as facts, but that isn't really true. ("Don't believe everything you think," says the wise bumper sticker.) In addition to experimentation, daily watering of our creative soil by others is, I'd argue, a second critical nutrient to my own mindset shifts.

As I was starting my business, it was my husband who offered me the most support and who challenged my own assumptions on a daily basis. When I lamented the lack of resources for new working parents in the world, he asked, "What are you going to do about it?" When I complained about feeling weird and awkward about selling something, he asked, "How can you help anyone if they don't know you exist? You do want to help people, right?" We are partners in life and caregiving, but also in prodding the other to think differently.

For me, it's the *daily* practice of receiving nutrients from others that matters. My husband and I have an ongoing conversation, but I've invited many other inspiring sources into my world, too. Seth Godin's daily emails help me start my day with a nugget of thought-provoking wisdom. "Don't say 'I won't,'" he recently reminded his readers, "say 'I haven't done that ★yet★.'" I'm always in the middle of a book (or two, or five!) that pushes me to think in new ways.

I work one-on-one with a therapist and a yoga instructor who help me challenge my assumptions and push me to stretch, both physically and metaphorically. I'm part of a founders mastermind group that holds space for vulnerability and new ideas. I'm part of a tight-knit group of Jewish mamas who meet monthly for ritual, safety, and friendship. These are the communities that water my soil.

WHITE SPACE HELPS THE SEEDS OF CHANGE GROW

Finally, I've found that the last of my mindset-changing gardening tactics involve a whole lot of nothing – doing nothing, that is. Counterintuitive, particularly in our culture? Yes. Immensely effective at shifting thoughts and moving mindsets forward, however? For sure.

In a world where I've been pandemic parenting for a year, I'll take any increment of so-called white space I can get my hands on.

On a daily basis, I practice yoga in the morning for fifteen minutes while using the free meditation app called Insight Timer. It's my space and time to just stretch and be in the world, and Insight Timer tells me I'm on a 500+ day unbroken streak. I don't consider a daily pause like this indulgent, but rather a life-sustaining practice.

On a weekly basis, my husband and I swap "alone time," where we each trade off the opportunity to be by ourselves and do something that nourishes us. I take three hours or so on Saturday afternoons, and he takes three hours or so on Sundays. It's impossible, I find, to let my brain reach new conclusions and try on ideas for size when I'm constantly in a state of *go, go, go.* Taking a few hours to wander the neighborhood, weed the vinca in front of our house, listen to an inspiring podcast, or even take a nap always leaves me seeing the world a little differently.

On a monthly basis, I've started taking a day off from work to re-group and go on a really long walk. In the midst of COVID burnout, I lamented to a close friend that I was close to breaking. She insisted I carve out this white space in my schedule, and then she held me accountable for taking it. (Yes, she made me text her the date I was planning to take off. After I took that day off, she asked for the next date!)

Finally, on an annual basis, my husband and I schedule planning days to look back, plan ahead, and imagine the futures we want to create. Yes, it takes work to carve out this time, but when else would we intentionally stop to pause and reflect?

In her glorious poem, "Fire", Judy Brown says, "What makes a fire burn / is space between the logs, a breathing space."

THE BLOOMING GARDEN

More than seven years into running my own business, I can look out and see that my gardens are growing. More than 1,500 new parents have taken the course I developed to support them in the transition back to work after parental leave. Eighty employers now offer the Mindful Return program to their new parent colleagues as a parental leave benefit. I've written a book, *Back to Work After Baby,* and co-host the *Parents at Work* Podcast. We just opened a UK Chapter of the Mindful Return program this spring, and launched a new training for managers of new parents.

This strikes me as a far cry from the risk-averse lawyer who was scared to write a blog post. But as I reflect back,

I note that there were no sudden shifts; rather, steady progress and constant baby steps. For me, the daily practices of experimenting, being supported, and remembering to pause are what matter. Like pacing in the dirt, sprinkling seeds with water from a watering can, these practices aren't particularly exciting, glamorous, or sexy. But they're truly what have allowed my own passions to grow.

LORI MIHALICH-LEVIN, JD, believes in empowering working parents. She is the founder and CEO of Mindful Return, author of *Back to Work After Baby: How to Plan and Navigate a Mindful Return from Maternity Leave,* and co-host of the *Parents at Work* Podcast. She is mama to two wonderful red-headed boys and is a partner in the health care practice at Dentons US LLP. Called a "working mama guru" by *Working Mother Magazine,* Lori has been committed to promoting women's equality and leadership throughout her career. Her thought leadership has been featured in publications including *Forbes, The Washington Post, New York Times Parenting, Thrive Global,* and *The Huffington Post.*

At Dentons, Lori advises health care clients on issues relating to graduate medical education reimbursement. She also founded and served for two years as the Co-Chair of the firm's parent and caregiver affinity group. Prior to joining Dentons, Lori worked as the Director of Graduate Medical Education and Hospital Payment Policies at the AAMC, and as a healthcare attorney at Vinson & Elkins, LLP and King & Spalding, LLP.

Lori holds a law degree from the Georgetown University Law Center and completed her undergraduate studies at Princeton University. Before beginning her health law career, she was a Rotary Ambassadorial Scholar in France, studying at the Institut d'Etudes Politiques d'Aix-en-Provence, and she served as a law clerk to the Hon. Neal E. Kravitz of the Superior Court of the District of Columbia.

PRACTICE WHAT YOU PREACH: FINDING JOY IN AUTHENTIC HUMAN CONNECTIONS

by Nicole Starr

Before I was a District Court Judge, I was a public defender. For ten years, I was part of a group of lawyers that saw ourselves as the justice league: brash and filled with bravado and bombastic. Our work, as I used to say, was God's work. I grounded my righteous indignation in the lives of poor, black, indigenous, and brown people. To say that I lived my job almost undersells the extent to which my work took over my life. Every moment of every day, I carried my clients, their families, and their sorrows with me. In my mind, every person's case could be won by a good lawyer, and I focused my energy and free time almost exclusively on what I needed to learn to be a better one.

Let me pause and reiterate: I believed that if I worked hard enough, every single case could be won. I carried this impossible imperative with me because I saw that every case was a human being. Every person deserved the best lawyer that not even money could buy, and that was me. As my yearly case numbers added up into the hundreds, this impossible dream drove me into a feeling of mania. My days were filled with courtroom slights made larger by the real and lasting effects of entrenched powerlessness, gut-wrenching poverty, and systematic racism. My thoughts were filled with my clients' desperation. In my head, I kept a running total of each casualty.

As the casualties grew, I carried a sense of hopelessness. But since I was the lawyer, hopelessness was simply not an option. Not only did I deny myself time to grieve and process, I also denied myself time to rest. There was always another crisis and another case that could be won by a good lawyer. So, instead of acknowledging that my heart ached for the people I served and the system to which I had sworn allegiance, I balled up that pain and turned it into anger, rage, and a cutting and deeply macabre sense of humor.

As I reflect, I am in awe of my ability to live in denial. My delusional sense of exceptionalism and belief that hard work could overcome any barrier warped itself into an intense hypervigilance surrounding my work. After my homicide trials, I began to imagine what people looked like dead. I ate lunch with one hand on a fork and the other holding crime scene photos. Every single love song was somehow twisted into the facts of any number of sexual assault cases. This all seemed completely normal because everyone around me was living an iteration of my story.

When I interviewed to become a judge, the commission asked me what I thought defines a good judge. My answer was this: "Good judges are emotionally regulated people. This allows them to listen not only to hear but to understand." Was I going to be a good judge?

Somewhere between getting fitted for my robe and entering my weeks of training, I realized that I had to reckon with the person I was and the person I aspired to be. I had to deal with the pain that I carried. To do this, I had to unbury ten years of pain that I had so carefully tucked away. My plan was to carefully and methodically uncover little bits of hurt and try to intellectually understand them. This worked about as well as opening a can of pop that has been rolling around the backseat of the car.

I started getting physically sick. At one public event, I thought I was having a heart attack and ran off stage. Another time, I left the bench in the middle of a plea hearing. It turns out that I had an anxiety disorder accompanied by panic attacks that left me gasping for breath, breaking out into a cold sweat, and physically unable to move.

I was in my first year of being a judge and I was immobilized by panic. I was enveloped in doubt about my ability to be a judge. I leaned heavily on my wife for support and assurance. Her brilliance and love gave me hope that I could do the necessary hard work.

My transition from lawyer to judge had a steep learning curve. There was the technical work, the legal study, and understanding the power and prestige of the role. But the hardest work was the self-reflection, and the emotional work to figure out how to be a person in power and not use old wounds and outdated ideals to recreate the system that I had so deeply critiqued. I stumbled, a lot, and started to engage with a new level of humility. I learned to be the student, not only the teacher, realizing that there was so much more to learn.

I gave advice every day. One of my judicial roles was to work in our treatment courts, data-driven courts that rely heavily on a public health approach to addiction and mental illness. Here, I gladly shared wisdom about the importance of self-care, slowing down, and finding balance. I reassured people that they had self-worth, that they were perfect as they were, and that the work we did in court was about unlocking potential and restoring people to their best selves. I actively used the power of the court to change behavior through listening to stories of sickness, encouraging meaningful connections, and suggesting personal changes that supported healing. I offered this to everyone, but myself. I had to learn to listen to my own advice. I had to shed my belief that I was somehow exceptional or different from everyone else.

Here are some of the pieces of advice I gave to folks in court but needed to hear myself.

SLOW YOUR ROLL

I often told folks in court to think about things BEFORE letting their enthusiasm lead them too quickly down a path that can cause them more harm than good, and yet I proudly displayed my merit badge of busy wherever I went.

I would look at my calendar and claim that I just could not fit another meeting in. I would look at my evening, finding myself so busy that I would eating dinner from a bag while driving between obligations. I said "yes" to everything, proud of being busy at the expense of what truly mattered: family, friends, and rest. For me, busy was shorthand for important, needed, and connected.

It is easy to say "slow down," but I felt like slowing down was causing me to lose my identity. I grieved the loss of busy. I felt guilty about resting. I slowed down in my role but then felt like I had so much time to fill. Sitting with that feeling became my most important mission.

ADD SELF-CARE TO YOUR SCHEDULE, AND STICK TO IT

I fought this one. I viewed my days as the endless adventures of winding rivers, and I the starry-eyed traveler, free-flowing and going wherever the day took me. Reality check: the starry-eyed traveler did not eat lunch, had coffee for breakfast, sat at a desk until her back hurt and could not use the full range of motion in her neck. So, I made a schedule. I stuck to it. It included post-it notes that said, "get up and stretch" and a full bottle of water to drink during the day. The schedule included a lunch break, and an end to the workday. For the first time, I took days off, and even spent time in bed, playing card games and reading trashy hilarious romance novels!

UNPLUG

I've often encouraged folks to turn off their cellphones. Everything shifted for me when I finally made the leap myself and took work e-mail off of my cellphone. I retooled one of my social networking sites to only show me pictures of smiling, hugging brown people who identify as LGBTQ+. I read the news once in the morning and stopped my habit of continuously refreshing my feeds. I turned my work computer off at the end of the workday.

Yes, I know this is not as radical as throwing my cellphone in a drawer and heading out to the Boundary Waters Canoe Area, but it was still something. As a constant connector, I felt like I was in the wilderness. I was in an unfamiliar place. It made me edgy and anxious. I knew I was missing out, and I was. Turning my cellphone off delivered a lesson in humility – as it turns out, nothing in my life requires me to respond at midnight. As my pastor told our congregation with love in her voice, "you are each special, but not THAT special."

PEOPLE, PLACES AND THINGS

This is a favorite AA saying about triggers. I knew other people who had friends outside of the law profession, but as my career and working habits intensified, my circle of non-lawyers became very small. More importantly, my tolerance for people who did not "think like a lawyer" became even smaller. Both of these beliefs, coupled with my inability to stop talking about death, crime, and violence, left me with a tiny social circle. In this tiny social circle, we took care of each other, but we also built walls of distrust toward people who did not see the world as we did. So when I took a theology class and another student sent me an e-mail saying that she enjoyed being in class with me, I thought she wrote those words as a class assignment. My world had become so jaded that I did not think someone would say something kind to me unless they had to or they wanted something from me.

Expanding my social circle grounded me, reminding me of the exhilaration and joy that comes from making emotional connections with others, in which I could share old hurts and find new places for growth. New friendships required new patterns, and in my new patterns, I felt inspired and magical. I could not contain my happiness. I wrote cards to people in nursing homes and people in prison. I imagined my missives to be tender messages of hope for lonely people. I reconnected with old friends and broke old patterns. I told them how much I love them and why. I asked about their hopes and their dreams. I shared mine.

With each conversation and each connection, my sense of wonder and beauty grew. The people I surrounded myself with awakened a part of me that I had forgotten. I uncovered that what brings me true joy is my connection to other people. My new circle brought me back to my roots and helped me realize that what made me a great lawyer and what makes me a great judge is my deep desire to form authentic human connections in an effort to support transformational life changes.

NICOLE STARR serves as District Court Judge for the Second Judicial District for the State of Minnesota. Prior to her appointment to the bench, she worked as an Assistant Public Defender for the Second Judicial District. Judge Starr clerked for the Honorable Justice Z. M. Yacoob at the Constitutional Court of South Africa. Judge Starr is a Witness Institute Fellow and attends the United Theological Seminary of the Twin Cities.

SHIFTING INTO THE SPOTLIGHT

by Kate Kerr

I love raising my hand for big, complex challenges, but I also fear the spotlight. As a kid, I always hid behind my mom's skirt, anxiously peeking out at the world. In school, I joined theatre to overcome this fear. However, while this helped me appear more externally visible, I was in character, being someone other than myself. I was still standing behind a mask.

As I got older, I craved impactful work, but I struggled because I did not want to be the spokesperson for those efforts. For example, several years ago, I had a chance encounter that led me to work behind the scenes of a big and meaningful project without being the face of it. I was at a meeting in San Francisco City Hall, and I overheard a woman in the hallway talking about her desire to build a shelter home for survivors of human trafficking in the Bay Area. Her vision for creating a safe home for women who had been trafficked aligned with work I had done on human trafficking advocacy efforts from a policy perspective as an attorney in Washington, DC., and in related work while on a U.S. Fulbright Scholarship.

While neither of those experiences prepared me for opening a domestic shelter home, I jumped in with two feet. I introduced myself and offered to volunteer.

Over the next several months, I quickly transitioned from volunteering to working full-time (and then some) for the organization. My role included raising funds, developing partnerships, building an organizational structure, and eventually recruiting and training staff. I was unprepared for launching a confidential shelter home that addresses complex needs, but I was comfortable asking for help and finding trained professionals to join the effort. I reached out to social workers, PhDs, therapists and other lawyers, collaborating to design the right model for the organization.

We interacted with countless people who told us that the project wouldn't work. However, within a year, the home was open and at capacity. Adequate funds had been raised with a reserve in place. We developed referral partners, created processes, and trained staff and volunteers. There were growing pains and mistakes, of course. However, in the face of doubts and naysayers, I was able to provide confident responses on how we would address challenges that were raised... even the ones we hadn't considered.

Going through that experience gave me confidence that I had skills to face the unknown and be a part of building something impactful. While I had accepted the role because I was still hiding behind someone else (the founder), I started to learn that I could make an impact.

LEADING OTHERS REQUIRES SELF-LEADERSHIP

After some time working in the shadows, I recognized that I wanted to make a bigger impact and felt I needed to develop into a leader who is willing to be at the front of an organization. If I wanted to lead, I needed to work on myself. I couldn't always stand in the shadow; I had to get comfortable with the vulnerability that comes with being in the spotlight.

I needed tools and skills to be a leader, confidence in facing the unknown without relying on a theatrical mask and self-belief that I could promote my vision as well as I could promote someone else's dream. I also wanted to be comfortable with accepting the rejection that comes with business development and entrepreneurship.

Over the course of eight years, I invested in my self-development so that I could step into leadership and ultimately start my own business. I took classes, had a coach, talked to entrepreneurs and cultivated a set of tools and a new perspective that allowed me to see the risk as an opportunity to grow and to challenge myself. I allowed myself to imagine being an entrepreneur without hiding behind a mask or someone else.

With time, I had the courage to be myself and at the front of my own business, Propelled Leadership LLC.

TESTING OUT MY TOOLS AND MINDSET

Starting was just the first challenge. After opening the business, I had to do the harder work of sustaining those thoughts when clients didn't immediately emerge or when a project didn't go as planned.

I had that opportunity to test out my new mindset early on in my business when I signed my first big, unknown client for a new workshop. I had done hours upon hours of research to add interesting content to the presentation. I worked with a graphic designer to have a great accompanying workbook and practiced the program.

Although I was comfortable delivering workshops (including virtual ones), I was nervous about this program because it was new content in front of a new client. I wanted everything to be perfect.

When the program started, my technology completely failed. The chat function was disabled. I couldn't open the breakout rooms for planned small group discussion, and the polls wouldn't launch. I took some of the technical difficulties in stride and adapted my course to bring interactivity into the larger group. However, I struggled to get participants to contribute much in the larger setting.

Then, as I introduced the new content, I could see that it didn't generate engagement. With my nerves in high gear, I developed a dry mouth, felt my ears turn pink and started skipping around content.

The result? The program was not as good as I had hoped.

What did I want to do? Hide.

Next thing I wanted to do? Stop advertising my programs.

These fears, and the "I'm not good enough" thoughts, could have stopped me from moving forward. While I knew I would face disappointments in this new business, here was the first time I needed to respond. I had to test my entrepreneur mindset and tools to move forward.

This first hiccup, while small, was a perfect one to practice on sustaining confidence. I incorporated several tools to do so, including naming those fears, exploring them by refocusing on my goal and vision, reminding myself of all the programs that I've successfully delivered, and breaking down next steps into bite-size actions.

NAMING

Naming is all about identifying those fears or "not good enough" thoughts. What do I mean when I say *name them?* While this looks different for everyone, I name my fears by writing a list. By writing them down, they seem less overwhelming. For me, those worries were:

- People hated the program and thought negatively about my skills.
- No one would come to the next session.

Becoming mindful of my thoughts gave me a starting place from which I could begin to explore and understand their impact.

EXPLORE

To explore, I took each thought and challenged it. I considered other perspectives, tested coach re-framing tools, and found an internal motivation to use that new perspective to move forward.

EXAMPLE

Old thought: People hated the program and wouldn't return.

Recognition of the limitations: I can't control what others think. There will always be people who do not like a program.

Reframe: The program wasn't bad – some people enjoyed it.

Support: There were some smiles. I had tested some of the content with peers, and they liked the content. I've received good feedback on prior programs.

Motivation: I want to succeed in this business. I will learn and move forward.

Each of these steps helped me explore my fears, test a new perspective and focus on my motivation. This approach didn't end my nervousness, but it allowed for more openness to other possibilities and action.

SMALL STEPS OF PROGRESS

Knowing that I was nervous about my next presentation to the group, I focused on the small steps that needed to be accomplished instead of focusing on the outcome I wanted. I listed the steps for content development and technology testing. I split each of these pieces into smaller ones, as little steps make the bigger goal more manageable.

Every day, I blocked off a portion of time to take a micro step to prepare for the presentation. Implementing these smaller chunks towards my goal allowed me to focus on the process rather than the outcome. In doing so, I had an opportunity to move forward at a pace that was doable for me.

CONCLUSION

I delivered my next presentation to that group and received great feedback on this second session. Being nervous about something new and challenging is okay. Making mistakes is part of the process. Learning to move forward after a mistake can be an opportunity.

KATE KERR, JD, ICF-ACC, SHRM-SCP, coaches successful professionals in developing the engagement, satisfaction and productivity they are seeking in their working lives. She is the founder of Propelled Leadership LLC, an author, speaker and executive coach.

With a background in strategic advisory services at Ernst & Young, a U.S. Fulbright Scholarship, legal practice at Orrick, Herrington and Sutcliffe and talent development at law firms, she has led teams in high profile talent initiatives in leadership development, performance management and recruiting. In addition to creating a Leadership Institute, she facilitates workshops on self-awareness, mindset, influence, communication, goal setting and action planning. She cares about people, their careers, development and overall engagement.

She has been active in the community, including as a Board Member of the Women's Foundation where she led the creation and deployment of a key initiative called the Workplace Employment Scorecard. She has served with several other nonprofit organizations in St. Louis and San Francisco.

Kate is a certified professional coach, holds a law degree from Georgetown University Law Center, completed her undergraduate studies at Grinnell College and received a Fulbright Scholarship in India.

At Propelled Leadership, she offers a 'Step Up' Leadership Development Program for associates preparing for partnership; a Lateral Integration program; and executive coaching focused on presence, self-awareness, influence and communication.

You can find more information about Kate here:
www.linkedin.com/in/kate-kerr
www.propelledleadership.com

LEADERSHIP REQUIRES SERVICE: A COMMITMENT TO THE SERVANT LEADERSHIP-PLUS PHILOSOPHY

by Yusuf Zakir

"If serving is below you, leadership is beyond you."

- Anonymous

I have a history of throwing myself into very challenging and unusual circumstances. Whether it was picking up and leaving Canada to move to California; leaving a successful law practice to work in diversity, equity, and inclusion; or demolishing my backyard to build a basketball half-court (Field of Dreams-style), I have a constant desire to move forward, strive for improvement, and shake things up.

However, I learned through experience that effective and long-lasting change comes through a philosophy I call "Servant Leadership-Plus." A servant leader shares power, puts the needs of individuals first, and helps people develop and perform as highly as possible. The plus-designation involves taking that leadership philosophy and adding to it by (1) truly caring for others; (2) serving as an example; and (3) working harder than you ever imagined.

This story is one example of my propensity to lead by serving.

I am a member of the Dawoodi Bohra faith. Dawoodi Bohra Muslims trace their heritage to the Fatimi Imams, direct descendants of the Prophet Mohammed (SAW). The Dawoodi Bohras throughout the world are guided by *al-Dai al-Mutlaq* (unrestricted missionary). Our present leader is the fifty-third al-Dai al-Mutlaq, His Holiness, Dr. Syedna Mufaddal Saifuddin (TUS). He serves as our leader, spiritual guide, and holy father. Most Dawoodi Bohra community members live in India, but over the last year fifty years, the Dawoodi Bohra population has grown significantly in North America.

I was raised in Toronto, where my father was heavily involved in managing the affairs of the Dawoodi Bohra community and in constructing the community's masjid (mosque). I moved to Southern California shortly after graduating university and quickly became engrained in the Orange County and Inland Empire chapter of the Dawoodi Bohra community. This chapter of the community is managed by a non-profit organization known as Anjuman-e-Qutbi (AEQ).

The community of AEQ was rapidly growing, with nearly 500 congregants spread out over several Southern California counties. In 2015, His Holiness inaugurated our new masjid, which would become the center of our community.

About a year later, I was appointed to help lead AEQ in the official role of Secretary. This appointment came as somewhat of a surprise to me and others in the community.

I was reluctant to take the role, but the directive came from His Holiness – and that, in and of itself, was reason enough to accept. Before my appointment, the community was led primarily by "elders" who had been serving the community for decades.

Being the Secretary of our community involved more than just taking minutes at a board meeting. Rather, it involved the responsibility of overseeing the entire administration. My primary responsibilities were to oversee the functioning of our programs and initiatives (e.g., a community kitchen program that serves 500 prepared meals a week); manage departments – including health, law, public relations, and finance – that provide support to our community members and our neighbors; and, of course, fundraise to help support it all.

There were several challenges I observed right away.

First, our faith is demanding. We meet frequently at the mosque, conduct significant community service programs, and are constantly striving to improve. His Holiness introduces initiatives to uplift our community and bring us closer to the faith, all of which require significant groundwork. In many ways, the community serves at the center of our lives. To be responsible for ensuring that this work not only continued, but dramatically improved, felt overwhelming.

Second, there was a generational gap. I was, by far, the youngest person to ever hold the post of Secretary in our community. There were many elders in the community who were initially skeptical of my ability to lead. At times, they could be patronizing and even condescending. They reminded me of their years of experience over mine and were resistant to any change.

Third, the level of active involvement in our congregation was weak. While our members regularly attended services, very few volunteered to help with wider initiatives. This challenge was exacerbated after my appointment. On countless occasions, senior community members handed their responsibilities over to me – things they had managed for more than a decade. I recall an individual who managed the maintenance and upkeep of the mosque handing me a thick binder with his only guidance being, "It's your job now."

Very quickly, I had to determine how to navigate these challenges and ensure that we could continue to steer the ship in a positive direction. For me, the path forward was to adhere to the philosophy of "Servant Leadership-Plus." This philosophy centers on service. The "plus" designation involves three additional components motivated by witnessing the effort of His Holiness: (1) truly caring for others; (2) serving as an example; and (3) working harder than you ever imagined.

TRULY CARING FOR OTHERS

To lead effectively, you must care for others – and you must do so genuinely. Caring is not and cannot be window-dressing. It has to be intentional, organic, and honest.

While this may seem obvious, it does not always happen. In leading any organization, there will always be multiple, competing, demanding priorities that require difficult decisions. In the face of speed and volume, it is far harder for us to make the time and space to be intentional. But, the moment we forget that people are our priority – and that caring for them is essential to leadership – we lose our ability to be effective.

In order to counteract this, you must actively carve out time for caring. This need not be complicated. For example, as I began to lead AEQ, it was critically important for me to show my support and dedication to my community members. It was particularly important because of the generational divide to show respect for those that came before me. I knew that my behavior and attitude were critically important and demonstrative, and could give others something to model. And so, I doubled down on caring. Tactically, this can happen in any number of ways, whether it is regularly checking in on someone (calling, texting, emailing); helping someone with a challenge they are dealing with; or just being generally helpful and available in their lives. I recall visiting an elder member of our congregation who was recovering from surgery in an assisted living community. I went to his home, spent some time with him, and helped him get some things organized at home. It was a small gesture, but it mattered.

SERVING AS AN EXAMPLE

To be engaged as a leader, you must be willing to do the work – not just the work of leadership, but work to support every aspect of the organization's efforts. This doesn't mean being a micromanager or hovering; rather, it involves empowering others and then offering to be of service to them.

Because engagement was thinning, our manpower was scarce. A small group of people ended up doing a great deal. This was not sustainable, particularly considering that His Holiness sought to elevate our congregations to new heights with innovative and ambitious programs. I needed to find ways to get more people actively involved. Most people did not have tremendous visibility into the administrative side of my role and the gears turning behind the scenes. I needed to set a visible example. One way in which I did that was to take on a lot of physical labor. For example, we had a number of date trees in our masjid complex and the dates would rot and fall to the ground. I would get down on my hands and knees to pick them up from the floor. Our commercial size trash can would overflow due to the volume of trash generated by our community kitchen program. I would re-organize the trash and clean out the area. I was willing to get my hands dirty.

These tasks were all things that needed to be done; I was not doing them for show. But by doing them myself, I was hoping to demonstrate that there was no task too small, too menial, too unimportant. Rather, every single task that anyone in the organization performs is critical and important. In addition to continuously emphasizing this fact, one must show it by pitching in.

WORKING HARDER THAN YOU EVER IMAGINED

With the acknowledgment that serving as an example is important, this comes with a consequence: you need to work harder than you ever imagined. You need to tap into an energy within you – an energy that you may not even know you have. There are instances in all of our lives where we are confronted with what feels like an insurmountable challenge. What we must realize is that to overcome it, we already have everything we need within us. In that instance when we first recognize the challenge, we may not believe it, and we may not believe in ourselves. Some may tend to opt out and succumb, and there's no judgment in that, but our spirit is deep and our abilities are limitless.

Like I said, our faith is demanding. To be in a leadership role within the faith is beyond demanding. I spent evenings and weekends at the mosque, supporting our people, efforts, and programs. This meant significant personal sacrifice. But I was trying to meaningfully pivot our organization in the face of concrete challenges, and I understood that this short-term sacrifice was necessary for the long-term health and success of our organization. This is particularly true in running a non-profit organization that operates purely on volunteer labor. I had to find a way to inspire others. Hard work is often an inspiration.

By adhering to this philosophy of Servant Leadership-Plus, I was able to lead and engage more people to get involved. In my first few years in the role, more community members – particularly, younger community members – joined our efforts. By serving them, they became more willing to serve others. This created a cascade of service, where more and more people became part of our efforts.

How does one get motivated to do all of this?

For me, it was the spirit of servant leadership, supported by the guidance of His Holiness. I put myself in the place of our community members. If I were in their shoes, what would I want of my community? And how would I want it to be led? If I could not meet and exceed that threshold, then I did not deserve to lead. And if I was going to take the mantle of leadership, then it was incumbent on me that I *actually lead*. By actively following the philosophy of "Servant Leadership-Plus" – to lead by serving – we can achieve the sustainable change that we desire.

YUSUF ZAKIR is the Chief Diversity, Equity, and Inclusion Officer at the national law firm of Davis Wright Tremaine. He leads the firm's efforts to continue building a culture where all attorneys and staff—including those traditionally underrepresented in the legal profession—can have, and can see, a path to long-term success.

He collaborates with key stakeholders to develop and implement strategies, programs, and initiatives to build a more diverse, equitable, and inclusive organization. He also partners with clients and external organizations in order to foster diversity, equity, and inclusion in the broader legal profession and to cultivate an industry that recognizes intersectionality, empowers authenticity, and nurtures belonging.

Yusuf is the father of two young children and is active in his faith community, including serving as secretary of a faith-based non-profit. In his spare time, he enjoys shooting hoops with his children.

FINDING YOUR COURAGE MUSCLE AND EXERCISING IT

by Danese Banks

Hi! My name is Danese and I am a "recovering attorney!" I mean that in the most respectful of ways. I'm still an attorney, just not a practicing one. Let me give you a little backstory: I am not one of those lawyers who knew when she was just a teeny, tiny tot that one day, she would grow up to become a big-time trial lawyer at a big-time law firm, working with all sorts of great and famous attorneys such as Johnnie L. Cochran, Jock Smith, and Samuel A. Cherry.

Nope. That wasn't my dream at all.

In fact, I remember wanting to be a dentist, a veterinarian, and then a doctor, until one fateful day when I saw a heart pulled out of a cadaver on a field trip – yuck! No, I wound up here because I happened to take a test during my first year in college that suggested I might be a good lawyer. So I majored in Political Science, graduated, and thought, *nothing else to do with a political science degree other than go to law school!* Lest, I digress.

I became an investigator after graduating law school and practiced law for more than twenty-two years. All the while, I still wondered what I wanted to be when I grew up and questioned if this was it. One day, I was finally able to answer that question with a big ole' NO! Now, I'm not knocking anyone who was called to practice law and feels like it's the bees knees. I have enjoyed my time as a lawyer and learned many things which are useful to me at this point in my life. However, practicing law for the rest of my life just wasn't for me.

So, at the height of my legal career, after working my way up to becoming a Managing Partner at a national firm, I called it quits.

I was forty-seven years old and decided, just like that, to start completely over.

For a year, I did absolutely and unequivocally nothing. I couldn't; I was just that tired. I was *beyond* tired; I was exhausted. I was *beyond* exhausted; I was burned out. I couldn't do anything. When people asked me what my plan was, I said, "Nothing. My plan is to do not one single, solitary thing." They were baffled. Heck, I was too! I hadn't saved up the money to simply do nothing, and yet, that's what I decided to do. Now, I wasn't independently wealthy, so I did have to take a few legal consulting jobs here and there to get by, but other than that, I rested. I played with my children. I spent time with my family. That, quite literally, was it.

I loved it! It was awesome. I could physically feel every cell in my body taking a deep breath, then finally exhaling, perhaps for the very first time. It was the best decision ever...until it was time for me to figure out my next move.

I'll never forget the day my husband came home, looked me dead in the eye, and said, "So now what? What are you going to do now?" I didn't like that question. I wasn't ready for that question. I hated the fact that he had the audacity to ask me that question. After all, he had spent the majority of his life playing for the NFL – his dream job! He had no idea how it felt to do a job that you didn't love or that you didn't have any passion for. Needless to say, the conversation did not go well.

In hindsight, though, it was necessary. It propelled me into my next step of becoming a certified professional coach. Something new, something foreign, the unknown. I had some experience with a life coach several years back and had been fascinated by the process, but I didn't think to become one until that conversation.

I was scared. I was excited. I was "scared-cited". I didn't know what to expect, and of course all of the "what ifs" started creeping in. What if I can't do this? What if I made or make a mistake? What if I'm not successful? And the worst, what if I'm not good enough? The list went on and on. I could talk myself both into and out of doing it on any given day.

But then, after doing some research – something us lawyers are conditioned to do – I decided to go back to school to become a coach.

During this time, the fear continued to creep in on all sorts of levels and on all sorts of things. And because I was attending a coaching school that insisted on coaching the soon-to-be coaches (aka me), I learned a lot about fear and how it shows up. You'd be surprised how tricky it can be. It can show up when we "play small" and don't do the things we are meant to do or desire to do. It can show up when we procrastinate because we are too scared to move forward with a particular project or idea. Even worse, it can show up when we completely talk ourselves out of doing the darn thing we came here to do.

Despite the many ways it can show up and the catastrophic damage it can do, in my journey, I have found that there are two very powerful yet simple steps that we can take to combat fear:

Step 1: Find your courage muscle.

Step 2: Exercise it.

How do you do this? There's probably all sorts of ways, but I will tell you the way that I did it; feel free to use it as well.

While on this coaching journey, I was exposed to all sorts of great coaches. I would bounce from one coach to another, looking for wisdom and information that would help me both personally and professionally. It was during this trip that I stumbled across Brendon Burchard, a high performance coach. I had heard of him before and thought he might be a motivational speaker of sorts but paid more attention to him this time around and realized he was much more.

He wrote a book called *High Performance Habits,* which highlights six habits that one should have if one wants to be a high performer in any aspect of their life. They are:

1. Clarity

2. Energy

3. Necessity

4. Productivity

5. Influence, and… (wait for it)

6. COURAGE

The book is also accompanied by an optional planner. Now, this is no ordinary planner. While it contains to-do list sections and space to plan every second of your day, it also contains a "Morning Mindset" and "Evening Journal" section. The "Morning Mindset" included ten questions, including Number Seven. Number Seven has changed my life.

It reads, "One thing I could do today that is a little outside of my comfort zone is to (try, ask for, express something, take a big step, etc.)…"

Every day that I opened the planner, I had to face Number Seven and think of something that I could do.

During the first couple of days, I left it blank. Another day, I wrote something down with a question mark next to it. Early on, I wasn't taking Number Seven seriously.

But then, after having to confront Number Seven day after day, I decided to really be open to it and do what it was asking me to do.

And the world just opened up.

One day, I wrote down that I would join a Facebook Group that I had previously been too intimidated to join. This one decision allowed me to meet a host of incredible women who are building or who have built seven-figure businesses.

Another day, I wrote down that I would monetize a skill that I had been previously using and giving away for free. This led to me making a considerable amount of money in something that I was just doing as a hobby.

Another time, it led me to really begin to focus on my business and develop a niche for coaching lawyers in their pursuit of life (creating a work/life balance), liberty (transitioning within and outside of the law) and happiness (leveling up in the legal profession).

I have only been doing this for a relatively short period of time, but I have countless examples of how this one question has helped me with specific projects, expedited my growth professionally and personally, and made the whole concept of fear LESS fearful.

I would be lying if I said I'm no longer scared or that I don't still have days where I can't or won't answer Number Seven. I don't know if fear, for any one of us, ever completely goes away. However, I can say that exercising that courage muscle – one task at a time, one day at a time, in both small and big ways – has made it less scary.

So, you don't have to buy the planner to ask yourself Number Seven.

Ask yourself daily: what can I do TODAY that is a little outside of my comfort zone?

What can I try? What can I ask for? What can I express? What big step can I take?

There will always be an answer and an exciting opportunity as the reward.

DANESE BANKS is the founder and CEO of The Life Changer Coach, LLC. She is both a Certified Professional Coach and Energy Leadership Index Master Practitioner who spends her time coaching people whose inner blocks and obstacles have gotten in the way of achieving their outer goals.

In her "previous career life," she was the Managing Partner of the Memphis office of The Cochran Firm, founded by the late Johnnie L. Cochran, Jr. She has been an attorney for over twenty-five years, practicing full time for over twenty-two years.

She retired from the practice of law in 2018, took some time off, and attended IPEC (Institute of Professional Excellence in Coaching) to become certified in coaching.

In addition to coaching, she also continues to use her law license as a mediator as well and has a separate mediation business. Both jobs provide her with the opportunity to serve people in the way she loves best – by solving problems and resolving conflict.

When she's not doing either job, she enjoys walking, dancing, being silly with her husband, two children and dog, traveling (pre and hopefully post COVID), and shopping. One day, when she fully grows up, she would also like to write children's books. You can learn more about her at www.thelifechangercoach.com and www.banksmediationservices.com.

SMALL SHIFTS MAKE BIG IMPACT

by Regan La Testa

L ife can be hard. Life can be stressful. We can allow ourselves to drop into a victim mindset or we can intentionally decide how to see the world. For too long, I looked at my adult life as though I had no control over anything.

However, I discovered along the way that while I cannot control everything, there are many things that I can control; especially how I view the world and my life.

To truly understand the benefits of the small shifts that I made to get to where I am today, it is important to understand where I was when I started making them. Admittedly, when I look back it was not pretty.

My husband and I got married the summer after I graduated from law school and immediately before I started a two-year judicial clerkship. Two years later, we welcomed our first daughter into our family. When she was eleven and a half weeks old, I began working as a bankruptcy attorney at one of the top law firms in the world. At the time, I *thought* this was my dream job and the pinnacle of law school aspirations. More importantly, I *thought* I could do it all: have the baby **and** the big career.

Perhaps under different circumstances, I could have. During my pregnancy, my husband decided to go to law school, and started his classes when our daughter was about six weeks old. He was working a full-time job with an hour commute time and going to school at night, which meant he was gone seventeen hours a day.

My husband wasn't the only one with lots to juggle: I was a new mom with a demanding new job and long hours. While I had help, I was generally doing it alone. I was tired and stressed. I spent many hours crying in my office.

After a year and half, my husband quit his job and went to school full-time. I felt that I had no choice but to continue working at the firm.

When our second daughter was thirteen months old, an amazing opportunity arose with the firm which allowed me to work from home without billable hour requirements. It was a win-win for both the firm and me. Nevertheless, while I was glad to be home with my girls, I constantly lived in fear that the firm would decide I was no longer needed and terminate me. I also felt that I had somehow let myself and my family down (my parents, especially) by not working full-time, becoming a partner at the firm, etc.

Despite the positive aspects of the arrangement, I often found myself living in a victim mindset and focusing on the possible negative outcomes rather than appreciating what I had. Of course, I didn't realize this at the time.

Years later, daughter number three was born. When she was four years old, she started having serious abdominal pain. There were numerous doctors' appointments and pickups from school. While these health issues resolved in less than a year, two years later I would be faced with the toughest years of my life.

Prior to 2014, my husband was happy with his career at the large firm where he was employed. However, he began working with a newly-hired partner who apparently had a bad reputation outside of the firm. This individual was difficult to work with, which placed a lot of stress on my husband. Up until that time, my husband had received phenomenal evaluations and reviews. Unfortunately, things shifted for him professionally as a result. My husband is a wonderful man and, like many men, sees his role in the family as the provider. As his position in the firm became threatened, so did his role as provider. He'd prided himself on supporting our family and being excellent at his job. As a result of the situation at work, he threw himself into his work and started to spend less time with me and our girls. Looking back, I suspect that he may have had a bout of depression. Nevertheless, at the time, his withdrawal had a massive effect on our family.

In some ways, I had to become both mom and dad to our girls. While their father was around, many times he wasn't always "present."

During this time, I was suddenly required to work seven days a week because a paralegal at my firm took unexpected family leave and left no directions for coverage of his work obligations. I was left to determine what needed to be done and when as well as looking for staff to assist in getting the work completed. To say that my mindset took a dive would be an understatement. The saving grace during the work crisis was my husband, who truly helped with whatever was necessary while I was working.

Once my work status returned to normal, the next disaster took place. In June 2015, we discovered that our heating and air conditioning units both needed to be replaced for an unplanned expense. Exactly two weeks after the installation of the new units, we came home at the end of the day to discover that our daughters' bathroom toilet had overflowed, causing major damage. For the next three months, I spent an extensive amount of time arguing with the insurance company and dealing with a forced renovation. The older girls were displaced from their bedrooms as a result of the flooding. My stress levels during this time were at an all-time high.

It was the first time in my life where I felt like I had no control over what was going on.

Little did I know that things were about to get worse, and my mindset, attitude, and stress levels would truly be affected at a level I'd never experienced.

Days after the work on the house was completed, my youngest daughter, a second grader at the time, complained of a headache and a sore throat. Antibiotics helped with strep throat, but it took six weeks, being diagnosed with chronic migraines, and a trip to the ER for IV medications before the headache ceased. The poor thing cried morning and night. The migraines became quite pervasive and disruptive.

The following year, my daughter missed or was sent home from school a total of twenty-seven days. Besides strep and migraines, she had an emergency appendectomy, among other things. The following year, she continued to suffer with health issues which required additional procedures and surgeries. All the while, my husband was still going through his own struggles, and we had two other children to care for.

My workload continued to increase, and I was generally working in the office four or five days a week. I cannot count the number of times I had to leave work to pick my daughter up from school, bring her to work with me, or attempt to work from home. Each morning, I would wake up without a clue as to what was going to happen that day. How would she feel when she woke up? Would she go to school? Would she stay at school? How was I going to get my work done? I felt alone. No one understood what I was going through. No one understood how out of control my life had become. And worse, I didn't know how to help my daughter.

One morning, I was in the parking garage before a court hearing, crying and screaming at G-d, asking what I had done to deserve everything that I was going through. Looking back, I recognize this as the definition of victim mindset: the idea that we have no control over what is occurring in our lives, that everything is happening **to** us, rather than **for** us.

I wish I could say that that was the day that my mindset began to shift, but it wasn't. It took a whole year before I started the ascent out of the despair I found myself in. The healing started with therapy, of which I am a huge proponent. In the beginning, though, therapy helped me to process what had taken place but I was still stuck in that victim mindset. During that time period, I often heard myself saying, "The problem is..." – followed by a reason why I took (or didn't take) an action or blaming someone else for what was going on.

Something really started to shift in be in the beginning of the spring of 2019. I was becoming stronger mentally. I joined a new gym and began exercising four to six times a week. My body was getting stronger too. After working with a career coach, it became clearer to me that I was not meant to be in the legal profession forever. Rather, my path and purpose were to help others who had gone through similar experiences as I had.

The irony is that only months before, I'd been researching what I needed to do to become a life coach. At that time, my fears, beliefs about money, time and my own ability as well as the thoughts of others prevented me from taking the steps toward my true purpose. It was only after the career coach validated what I intuitively knew that I moved forward with my coaching certification. Even then, despite the changes I had already begun to make in my mindset, I still felt like I needed validation.

Shortly after that, I felt a true shift and found myself less and less in a victim mindset and more and more in one of agency, by choice.

So how did I make that shift? While my process may not be novel, it is one that worked for me.

VISUALIZATION

I visualized, in writing, what I wanted my life to look like in ten years. I envisioned BIG. I envisioned specifics. Most importantly, I envisioned my future in the present tense, as if it had already happened. Instead of "I want to have a vacation home," I would write "I have a vacation home at the beach where my family spends summers." Instead of "I want to be a great coach," I would write "I have a thriving coaching practice with a waiting list of future clients." When I could see it, I could begin to feel it, and then I could begin to believe it would happen. Believing that I could obtain the life I envisioned helped me take ownership of my life and realize that I do have control over my thoughts, actions/reactions, and beliefs. This shift alone allowed me to transition into an agency mindset. Even now, when I feel myself slipping into that victim mindset, I go back to look at my ten-year vision and, occasionally, revise it to encompass any new changes to my vision.

GRATITUDE JOURNAL

Every morning, I would write down five things for which I was grateful in the preceding twenty-four hours. Requiring myself to journal daily about things that made me grateful compelled me to become aware of those things. I also began to look for things that brought me gratitude. This practice helped me realize that even when things aren't going the way I want them to, there are always at least five things that I can appreciate from the day. Sometimes coffee would make my list. And that's okay! Finding gratitude isn't always about listing the most profound parts of life. As long as you find something to be grateful for (no matter how small), you are on the right track.

A gratitude journal helped with my mindset shift because I trained my brain to view things from a different perspective and realize that not everything going on in my life was bad. This awareness alone allowed me to begin to take control of my life and make things happen on my own terms.

SLEEP

When things were at their worst with my husband and my daughter's health, I couldn't sleep. How could I? There were so many things running through my head. A big shift I made as I began to regain my power was that I started prioritizing sleep. Even as a child, I knew lack of sleep had a profound effect on how I felt, thought, and behaved. This still holds true today. When my sleep is negatively impacted, I'm less in control of my actions and thoughts. I get migraines. I'm crabby.

Once I started making sleep a priority, by getting into bed at a reasonable time, putting away electronics, and, admittedly, taking melatonin on occasion, I found that I had an increased ability to choose my reactions, thoughts, and feelings. Once I was able to choose how I reacted as well as manage my thoughts and feelings, I found myself feeling less and less like a victim. Instead, my perspective shifted into one of agency and control.

EXERCISE AND HEALTHY EATING

As I moved into this new chapter of my life, exercising and making healthy food choices became a bigger priority. For me, I know that my eating gets "out of control" when I am not feeling good about myself. Eating healthy foods makes me feel better both physically and mentally. Similarly, exercise helps to keep my anxiety and depression under control. When I am moving my body along with feeding it well, my mood improves and am better able to make mindset shifts as needed.

When I focus on my health, I feel better and think clearer. As a result, I am able to see things in a better light. I can analyze circumstances from a more positive perspective. Just like with sleep, these lifestyle changes allow me to guide my thoughts, reactions, and feelings in a more productive direction. All of this leads to me being in a state of agency, rather than in victim mode.

The more I practiced these four actions, the more I realized that more than just my mindset needed to change. One of those things was my career. For so long, I had felt that I was working to work. I'd lost my passion for what I was doing. Deep down, I had known for a while that I wasn't living my true purpose, which was to serve others. As part of my mindset shift, I finally stepped into my purpose and took action. I knew it was time to choose who I wanted to be and make decisions accordingly.

You don't always need to make big changes to shift your mindset. Sometimes, even seemingly small adjustments can make a huge difference in your outlook and how you see yourself. For me, the four actions outlined above helped me to see the bigger picture. By taking the reins, I saw my true capacity to take ownership of my life and move from victimhood to true agency.

REGAN K. LA TESTA is a "recovering" attorney who spent twenty years in the bankruptcy practice group at DLA Piper LLP (US) before making a career shift to coach working parents (i) to stop operating out of overwhelm and self-sacrifice and to step into the fulfilling life they desire and (ii) to make changes in their nutrition and fitness to improve their health and well-being. She is the founder of Green Lava Coaching, LLC, an author, and a coach.

Regan is a Certified Professional Coach, a Master of the Energy Leadership Index Assessment and Specialist in COR.E Dynamics for Leadership, Wellbeing, and Transitions, each of which were obtained through the Institute for Professional Excellence in Coaching ("iPEC"). Additionally, she received her PN Level 1 Certificate in Nutrition and Coaching from Precision Nutrition and her Certified Personal Trainer certification from ISSA.

When not working, Regan enjoys volunteering in her community, exercising, reading, and spending time with her husband, three daughters, and two dogs.

Learn more about Regan La Testa and Green Lava Coaching at greenlavacoaching.com.

THE ENOUGH BOX

by Rebeka Garcia Cook

C ar batteries.

Its original purpose was to carry car batteries. Six of them, to be exact.

True to form, it is constructed out of heavy-duty cardboard. It is almost too heavy to lift alone; I can't imagine how heavy it was when it carried car batteries.

I've had the box for many years – a practical contribution from a friend when I moved many years ago.

All of the other boxes from subsequent moves have always been broken down and passed on, but this one – this one – has stayed. It has stayed for almost eighteen years.

The box currently resides in our family laundry room, its home for six years. In our previous house, and the house before that, it lived in the front coat closet. In every home, a black plastic trash bag lines the sturdy sides of the box. A roll of bags wait ready under the gaping bag.

This is my "enough" box.

Both my parents grew up in poverty. Their parents before them were immigrants and children of the depression. My grandparents kept things; after all, those things might be needed. They worked hard, they were careful, they used and reused items, they sometimes did without, and over time – and with much sacrifice – the American dream became a reality for them.

My own childhood began with the economic tightness of my parents starting their own business. They were also careful with their money and how they spent it. They were frugal. Like their parents, my own parents had learned to hold onto things. In time, and with much hard work and sacrifice, their business thrived.

Yet my parents continued to be careful with their money...and they continued to hold onto things.

As an adult, I did the same. I worked hard, I was careful with my finances, and I held onto things.

That was until my husband and I combined households. I had stuff: good stuff, helpful stuff, but some of it was stuff I didn't need. And now with adding his stuff, we had double stuff.

Together, we did the hard work of passing things on. In the process, I realized there was an unintended consequence of my parents' and grandparents' frugality: would I have enough?

That question and its siblings – "am I enough?" and "did I do enough?" – bred uncertainty in me. And I realized it was that uncertainty that caused me to be afraid and to hold on to so many things.

I kept things because I was afraid – afraid of what would happen if I didn't keep them, afraid I wouldn't have enough, afraid I wasn't enough, and afraid I couldn't do enough.

On the surface, I looked wise, frugal, and diligent, but inside of me was a different reality. I became curious: how did this good and helpful behavior get so twisted?

I realized every item I kept was a shackle holding me to a scarcity mindset and reinforcing the idea of "not enough." For clarity, my reckoning was not a dramatic event or a situation that required a massive dumpster. It was not pathological. Rather, my "stuff" was well within bounds of normal living. But *in me,* holding onto things was being driven by fear, and to overcome the fear of not enough, I needed to trust that I had enough.

So we began to pass things on. The initial clean-out happened naturally as we combined two households, moving from "me" to "we." The box was set up shortly after because we found that there continued to be double and excess.

One double that led to much internal consternation was between two cheese slicers. I prefer a solid metal slicer – a cheese plane is the official name – while my husband brought an adjustable wire slicer into our new, tiny family. The scarcity voice in my head shouted, "Keep both! We might need both styles. It would be awful to replace something you gave away. What if one breaks?" These thoughts protected me from uncertainty. This moment was a pivotal one. Would I listen to the concerned voice of lack?

My thoughtful voice replied, "I despise wire cheese slicers, and I can spend $5 to purchase a new one – $15 if I want a specific, more expensive one. I don't need two, I don't want two, so I will make a choice and I choose my cheese plane." The adjustable slicer went into the box. Guess what? My husband didn't like wire cheese slicers either! I started to accept that I had a scarcity mindset, but realized it didn't have to stay as a scarcity mindset.

This is how we use the box today; it sits in the washroom, trash bag in, ready to receive.

As we go about living, we drop things in the box that are still usable to others: shirts that fall out of favor, outgrown children's clothing, the pen drawer that is overfilling, toys that no longer bring delight, or read books.

Enough is anything we can share, anything we no longer need, or something someone else can use.

About once a month, the box is filled to capacity and is taken to a donation station.

For my three children, passing things on is their normal. One January, my daughter brought an arm load of stuff down the hall and, unceremoniously, dropped it into the box. I noticed there was a doll she got for her birthday in October and a toy she got at Christmas. I quickly pointed this out to her and she responded, "Mom, I've played with them. I have other toys I really like and I am ready for someone else to use these now." She has enough.

How about you? Do you have a scarcity mindset around having, being, or doing enough? Can it be different for you, too? Yes!

First, identify and accept that a scarcity mindset is a part of your *current* thinking. "Not enough" can be persistent across many areas but it is usually focused on one of these three areas: having, doing, or being. Which of these three is most prevalent for you?

Next, be curious about your feelings of "not enough." I wonder why you feel you are not enough. Journal your responses or talk it out with a safe person. Hold off judgement, invalidation, or minimizing your reasons. Just accept it – your reasons are your reasons. As you reflect on "not enough," you will discover a story. The story is how your brain makes sense of your experience in relation to all of your other experiences.

Sit with your story. There are three things to consider:

1. What are your identity statements?

2. Is there a comparison happening?

3. Does your story bring you shame?

IDENTIFY IDENTITY STATEMENTS

Identity statements are places where you have adopted an "I am" statement. Identity statements are important because there are actions that flow from identity. "I am a bad public speaker." "I am never finished at work." "I am ugly." "I am not very smart." Test these identity statements. Are they true? Are they always true? Is this identify item actually a skill that can be developed? And you are judging as permanent something that has not yet been developed? If you are still unsure, ask others. Pay special attention to identity statements that seem permanent, pervasive, and personal; these have a deep foothold and are likely untrue.

COMPARISON

Are you comparing yourself to someone or some ideal? Seeing something you do not have creates three types of responses: disinterest, a desire to have "it" as a means of increasing your happiness based on the premise that obtaining it will make you more worthy, or an aspiration to have something the same or similar. Disinterest doesn't really impact you; likely, you forget what you saw. The second two are more powerful, one in a helpful way and one in a condemning way. If the comparison spurs you to greatness and awakens a fire of passion and delight, go for it! Unless obtaining the "it" is meant to validate your self-worth. Dear reader, a sense of worthlessness or not enoughness can be fought by giving. Too much to do? Give some time away; volunteer. Don't think you are worth anything? Give away your expertise; you've got some. Don't have enough stuff? Share or give away what you do have. You will be amazed at how much value you bring to the world and how suddenly you realize you do have, and are, enough.

SHAME

Brené Brown defines shame as the "intensely painful feeling or experience of believing that we are flawed and therefore unworthy of love and belonging." Do you recognize a sense in yourself that this "lack" is something that other people would reject you for? That feeling is shame. Thankfully there is an antidote to shame: connection. Share your story with others (safe ones!) and let them see you and accept you. Yes, even that story – you know the story I am talking about. It is your version of spending an excess amount of time trying to make a decision about a $5 cheese slicer.

Is it realistic? Oftentimes, the image of our desire – our not enough – is not realistic. Several reasons are: (1) the image is the result of a specialization far beyond what most people could realistically give of themselves; (2) you are seeing a photoshopped or social media-ready version of reality and what you see is not the whole story; and (3) you are seeing the result of many people's work, not just a single person.

Next, decide what story you want to tell. You cannot change the events, but you can interpret the meaning of the experiences. "I messed up royally and will never amount to anything" can be reframed as, "I messed up that time and I am learning." Reframing your story takes a single instance and places it into a larger story. The story is not over; the "not enough" was just one experience. As you rewrite your story, include situations where you demonstrated your power, where you exercised agency. Owning what you did, as a choice, is empowering as well. What might other perspectives be that you can consider when rewriting a story? Finally, rewrite your story.

My daughter approaches stuff much differently than I do. She has a different approach to looking at stuff. In her, I was able to shift her mindset faster than in me, but I am also making a shift in my own mindset with effort and practice. I've realized several things because of my box.

I have enough. Rarely have I needed (or wanted) something I've passed on. I am much more aware of my likes and desires because I keep the things that bring me pleasure. This means that I am much more aware of who I am and what brings me joy. Also, my kids are much more aware of their likes and needs because of the box. I am regularly reminded that my needs are all met.

Additionally, I have more than enough; I have enough to share. I have good things that I can share with other people. Not everyone wants my things, but someone does, and it will be a good thing for them. That fact reminds me that *I am* enough, even if I am not for everyone.

Sometimes, I throw something in the box that could use repair; perhaps a button is missing, and guilt for not passing on a perfect item begins to well up. Then I remind myself that what I am doing is enough. I cannot do everything. I am a person who has real limits. My limits help me prioritize. They direct my energies so that my vision can become a reality. I am doing enough.

My box affirms daily that there is enough, you are enough, and you are doing enough.

REBEKA GARCIA COOK, MPH, is a certified executive coach who specializes in helping female business and organizational leaders create the future they desire in the systems that matter to them.

These leaders care deeply and are passionately involved in their businesses, families, and communities, and desire fullness in all of these areas. They are most at peace when transforming their world- their systems- by using their gifts and resources to impact the things that matter deeply to them. However that passionate heart can also create a frenzy that is exhausting and demanding and robs the joy from work and life. Rebeka helps clarify what is most important and supports them as they align and focus their energy to continue to transform the world and enjoy life while doing it.

Rebeka helps change and transformation happen faster, fuller, and more sustainably by coming alongside them to clarify, listen, contain, propel, and encourage them as they create their desired future.

Rebeka's Intentional Vision kit can be downloaded, free, at:
www.greenboatcoaching.com/join
Email: Rebeka@GreenboatCoaching.com
Web Page: www.GreenboatCoaching.com
LinkedIn: www.linkedin.com/in/RebekaGarciaCook
Facebook: www.facebook.com/GreenboatCoaching

ALL VIBES WELCOME

by Yashar Khosroshahi

I t was 10 p.m. I was alone in my car in an empty parking lot.

My hands were wrapped around my throat; I was squeezing as hard as I could. I'd never felt so determined to harm myself.

I was desperate. I wanted the whirlwind of painful emotions to just...stop.

My wife and newborn were at home asleep, and my wife had no idea where I was.

Tears were streaming down my face. My body felt tight, and my breath was short.

I felt lost, overwhelmed, and angry, but most of all, I felt ashamed, stupid, and weak.

For most of my life, I can remember waves of darker emotions coming over me. I recognize this pain as "feeling disposable."

Between the ages of three and twenty-three, I moved from Tehran, Iran, to Birmingham, Alabama, to Scarborough, Ontario, just to name a few of the moves. In total, I attended eight different schools in seven different cities during that time.

Each time there was a change, I felt like I was being uprooted. I felt like the process of knowing who I was, where I belonged, where my home was, and that I mattered started all over again.

Throughout the years, I found different ways to prove to myself, and to my new surroundings, that I wasn't disposable.

In grade school, I discovered I could mask my pain by making people laugh; I was the class clown. In high school, I turned my focus to athletics. In university and medical school, it was academics, and I found what I thought was my perfect drug: achievement.

Doing more, and being recognized for it, was a security blanket. Achievement gave me a high and would temporarily soothe my pain. Achievement hid my distress and presented the more polished side of me. But above all, I believed that the greater my achievements, the greater my chances of feeling valued and desired were, and the quicker my darker vibes would dissipate.

Months before that night in the car, this line of thinking started catching up to me. I had given up my general practice (and the majority of my family's income), started a new business, and become a first-time parent. And for the first time, maybe ever, I couldn't figure out how to achieve fast enough to soothe my pain.

During this time, I also started becoming acutely aware of how our society glorifies the mantra "positive vibes only." It seemed to be posted everywhere.

This mantra is so enticing – and presumably the best way to live. But what "positive vibes only" is saying is that when we feel any other vibe, we're not welcome in the club, and we need to return to positive vibes as quickly as possible. And this mantra definitely doesn't leave room for feeling ashamed, stupid, and weak.

I can vividly remember the violent discourse and disenchanted feelings that coursed through me sitting in that car. I kept thinking, *I should have healed my pain by now!* I thought that if I worked hard enough on myself, and for others, I'd be free from the darkness I knew so well!

As this familiar, deep pain started to reappear, I felt like a failure, despite doing all the "right things," reading all the "right books," and stacking up all the "right degrees."

In that moment, I no longer wanted to hear my pain's voice. I kept my hands wrapped around my neck with no real plan, and as I began to feel short of breath, I heard a voice from within me ask, "are you really sure this is the only way to face your pain?"

The timing of that question did more than just surprise me. It forced me to consider what I have never fully admitted to myself. With that one question, it was like all the years of achievements and trying to prove to the world that I wasn't disposable came crashing down to reveal one absolute truth: *I don't know how to love myself through my darkest emotions.* It became very apparent that it was time for me to take my own medicine in a deeper way than ever before.

You see, pain is that person who will walk through your front door uninvited, go through your fridge and closet, make itself comfortable on your couch, eat your snacks, and hog the remote control. You can change your locks as many times as you want, but pain always finds the key somehow.

Here's the deal: sustainable peace and safety don't come from trying to lock pain out. They come from understanding pain in a very different way.

I needed to build a whole new relationship with my emotional pain. I needed to learn to *connect* with my pain before I tried to *correct* my pain.

I needed to accept my pain as a demanding teacher and not my enemy. This meant that I needed to start *letting* it in instead of *blocking* it out. I needed to start *talking* to it instead of *silencing* it. I needed to *sit still* with it instead of *running away* from it.

Pain knows better than to just walk away before we have learned what we're supposed to learn. Pain places challenges before us to build a deeper understanding – of ourselves, our family, our community, and the world. Pain is asking us to deconstruct the "positive vibes only" mantra and to rebuild an "all vibes welcome" relationship with ourselves.

A relationship like this has to start by accepting a simple truth: as humans, we are in a lifelong relationship with emotional challenges. They will never conveniently "go away." Pain will come and go, and have its seasons, but in order for us to grow, we must *welcome in* and *make meaning* of each and every one of our vibes.

So how we do this? What is at the core of "all vibes welcome"?

SELF-COMPASSION.

Now, I know self-compassion can get some eye rolls. It can sound pretty fluffy. As you read this, you may even be thinking that this is the type of feel-good message one says when there is no real evidence or science to deal with emotional distress.

I thought this too – for years – as I tried to fight my way through my darker vibes, but we all need self-compassion! It's the friend whom emotional pain keeps crying out for.

According to a rich body of scientific literature, self-compassion is one of the most robust tools available from a psychological and neurological standpoint. When practiced consistently, it activates the brain's innate ability to respond more accurately, and in a deeply personal and meaningful manner.

Over time, the more I worked with self-compassion – personally and professionally – the more I came to appreciate it as a state of thinking and feeling, one that prepares an individual to take positive, empowered, and deliberate action. There is nothing automatic or easy about this state of being, but it is a fundamental ingredient for sustainable growth and healing.

Self-compassion has the power to create an internal sense of safety so that we can learn to be both vulnerable with our experiences and our vibes, and also accountable to our well-being.

So how do we do this? How can each of us cultivate self-compassion?

It starts with a conversation.

Self-compassionate conversations can take on many forms and go many layers deep. No conversation will ever be exactly the same.

But that night in my car, in the middle of my messy and chaotic thoughts, a confused heart, and a continual downpour of tears, there were three questions that stood out from all the noise.

Although I have refined these questions over the years, they are the same questions I asked myself that night, and I continue to ask myself every time I'm experiencing challenges.

Q1: HOW WOULD I APPROACH A LOVED ONE IN THIS SITUATION?

I first imagined how I would approach my sister in this same situation. Then I thought, *what if my best friend was sitting here next to me grabbing his throat?* And finally, *how did I approach my patient from earlier this week who was contemplating suicide?*

None of my answers included dismissal or violence. All of my answers included connection, understanding, compassion, space for imperfection, and a place for all their vibes.

In that moment, I recognized that my pain has always been asking for my friendship. It was telling me to have the courage to be compassionate towards myself. I realized I was more deficient in loving myself than I was desperate for others to love me. I am more deficient in accepting and welcoming all my vibes than I am desperate for positive vibes only.

We often do more and show more patience and compassion for others whom we care about than we do for ourselves. But your pain wants your friendship, too. This means we must learn to start *connecting* to our pain before we try to *correct* our pain.

Q2: WHAT IS ONE STEP I CAN TAKE TOWARDS SUPPORTING MYSELF?

I knew I couldn't fix all my pain in that one moment in the car, so I focused on taking a baby step. My step was a very crucial one: to stop harming myself. My focus remained there. I wasn't asking myself to solve the problem; I was asking myself not to add to the problem, because that was the most self-compassionate thing I could think of doing in that one moment.

I know it's tempting to wish away all of our suffering, to want it to vanish instantaneously, but sustainable change occurs over time. By focusing on taking one step towards supporting ourselves, we are initiating the first ripple towards sustainable health. We must learn to honor these micro moments in our individual journeys because they are the building blocks that lead to macro changes, and a more solid relationship with ourselves and others.

Q3: HOW CAN I TELL THIS STORY OF MY PAIN DIFFERENTLY?

My story of feeling disposable continued to exist within me because I have only tried to dispose of the story of my pain. I had never considered using my pain to recover a deeper sense of love for myself.

Later that evening, as I laid in bed next to my sleeping wife, I still felt shattered and scared.

I felt far from perfect, but by listening to the story of my pain more carefully, I was home safe, and I was choosing self-compassion for what my pain was telling me.

We can all learn to tell the story of our pain with an emphasis on recovering and repairing our strained relationship with ourselves. We no longer have to worry about perfecting ourselves.

Our challenge, therefore, is not which vibes are good or which vibes are bad, but how can we welcome in self-compassion for an opportunity to transform? Self-compassion is the catalyst to change the story of our pain so that we can honor the parts of us that we've neglected.

These questions allow me to honor my struggle and all my vibes.

How differently would you feel if you embraced all your vibes?

What would change if we welcomed all vibes in our homes, schools, workplaces, and communities?

Pain asks us to sit up and pay attention, and therefore we must not judge or dismiss its calling.

Pain places a spotlight on the parts of us that we keep in the dark, the ones we reject and avoid, and that is exactly why it possess the instructive power to enlighten us.

Emotional challenges may act as a destructive force, but they're also evolutionary, and that is exactly why they have the power to transform us.

In a culture where we chase happiness and display filtered images of ourselves and our lives, there's seemingly little room for imperfection as we glorify "positive vibes only." But the dark times live within all of us, and we can't just hashtag and swipe our pain away. So let's embrace pain as a great teacher and a pathway to newfound insights and strength.

Let's honor the dark so we may revel in our light.

By creating the space for us to be our whole selves, we are cultivating a home for our best selves. All vibes welcome teaches us the art and science of emotional transformation. It teaches us to *connect* to our pain before we *correct* our pain.

DR. YASHAR KHOSROSHAHI, ND (inactive), ACC is a Naturopathic Doctor, Mental-Emotional Strength Expert, Certified Brain-Based Executive Coach, and the co-founder of **MIND***SHIFT* LEADERSHIP, a leadership development firm. He trains high-performing leaders to strengthen their mental-emotional foundations through mindset coaching.

He is a TEDx speaker on the power of self-compassion, a featured guest in Dr. Mark Hyman's Broken Brain Series and teaches Health Psychology at the Canadian College of Naturopathic Medicine. Yashar leverages his experience as a Naturopathic Doctor to help leaders optimize their performance while prioritizing mental health.

THE ONLY WAY OUT IS THROUGH

by Kendra Brodin

I start most days with a full reserve of motivation and a feeling that I can conquer the world. I get up each morning and make out a bright, shiny daily plan, but throughout the day things happen that slowly cause my "motivation faucet" to turn off. My to-do list feels longer at the end of the day than when I started, and new projects pop up when my plate already feels full. Sometimes one of my three kids gets sick at the worst possible moment or has a last-minute school deadline (that they conveniently forgot to tell us about). Other times, my husband and I find ourselves triple-booked with various work and family commitments, despite our best planning efforts. Cars break down, the internet goes out, or the furnace stops working. On top of life's unexpected occurrences are my continual aspirations to work out more, declutter my space, spend more time cooking, and so on.

Happy thoughts don't cut it when it comes to the intense waves of overwhelm, insecurity, frustration, anxiety, and inadequacy. Instead of feeling motivated, all I want in those moments is a bag of corn chips, a bowl of guacamole, and a remote control so I can binge-watch Netflix.

Over the years, I have learned that when I lose my motivation, something in my thinking is "off." As a certified coach, I use the same coaching techniques and frameworks I use with others on myself. Why? Because these strategies allow me to reset my mindset and recover my motivation.

Here is what makes the difference for me when my motivation wanes: as part of my coach training, I learned how to manage my mind and help others do the same. Ultimately, I realized that I'm in control of whether I feel motivated or not, as my motivation is based on my thoughts, and my thoughts are my responsibility.

If I'm not feeling motivated, then I need to look at my own thinking and ask myself why I am putting off what I know I need to do. If I'm being honest with myself and looking deep inside, I usually uncover that don't want to do the tasks I need to do because I'm trying to avoid some feeling of discomfort.

Maybe I don't want to write the memo, brief, or article that is due tomorrow because I'm afraid of failing.

Maybe I don't rehearse for the presentation I have next week because I'm afraid of somehow embarrassing myself. If I can tell myself that I didn't really practice, then maybe I won't feel so bad about myself if the presentation isn't amazing.

Maybe I feel insecure and worried about being judged, so I don't sign up for the committee or leadership position I know I would enjoy and that would give me some additional credibility and visibility.

Maybe I don't want to feel the physical pain of a new workout regime, so I put it off and break promises I've made to myself about working out more.

Maybe I don't want to risk hurting someone's feelings or speaking my truth and causing awkwardness, so I avoid having the hard conversation with the colleague, family member, neighbor, or friend who said something out-of-line or did something that hurt me.

Maybe I am nervous about how others will perceive me in a social situation, so I try to come up with reasons to skip the networking event.

When I stop to think about all of these situations, I realize that the situations themselves (e.g. writing a memo, starting a new fitness plan, attending the networking event, cleaning my storage room, etc.) are completely neutral. They don't have a positive or negative charge until I think about those situations and load them up with meaning.

Circumstances are situations that are typically beyond our control. Even though we can't control them, the circumstances themselves are always neutral until we attach our thoughts to them.

Thoughts have the power to motivate or demotivate. Our thoughts about our circumstances are what matter. When "life" happens (the "circumstance"), our minds immediately want to think thoughts about that circumstance, and the thoughts we think make all the difference. The good news is that we can always control our thoughts. It's never the circumstances that cause our feelings, but our thinking about the circumstance. Thoughts cause feelings.

Feelings are vibrations in our bodies (i.e. feeling sad, happy, confident, rejected, excited, frustrated, or anxious). Feelings drive behavior. When you have feelings, take a deep breath and figure out what thought caused the feeling. I promise there is a thought behind that feeling, and that thought either empowers or disempowers you.

Actions are what we do – or don't do – based on how we feel. Our feelings incite us to take action (or sometimes, to avoid acting) based on our current feelings. If we feel confident and excited about something, we are likely to act. If we are feeling worried, frustrated, angry, or resentful, many times we avoid acting in ways that would move us closer to our goals.

Results are the effects of our actions. Our results are usually the logical outcome of the actions we've taken. Amazingly, our results often give us evidence of our initial thought.

That's it – that's the coaching framework that I use to coach myself and others. It's so simple, but it's not always easy. We are socially programmed to believe that things just happen to us and that we have no control over our thoughts or feelings, but that simply isn't true. Each of us has complete control over our thoughts. We aren't at the mercy of our unconscious thinking or simply reacting to the world around us. We each create our feelings, actions, and results with our own thinking. This is so empowering because it means that we can create motivation with our thinking as well.

Here's an example of my thought process about writing a memo when I'm lacking motivation.

Circumstance: (What is objectively happening right now?) The memo is due at 5:00 p.m. tomorrow.

Thought: (What am I thinking about the circumstance?) I don't want to write the memo because I'm afraid it won't be good enough.

Feeling: (How do I feel when I think this thought?) I feel discouraged.

Action: (What action am I taking, or not taking, based on how I feel?) I procrastinate, find other things to do, and put off writing the memo.

Result: (What is the result of my actions when I think this thought?) The memo doesn't get written.

But, of course, this isn't the result I want. I want to feel motivated. I want to write this memo, feel proud of it, turn it in, and feel relief and pride for getting it done. What would I need to think instead and how would that change things?

What if I changed those de-motivating, disempowering thoughts to thoughts that actually got me moving and got me the results I want?

Circumstance The memo is due at 5:00 p.m. tomorrow. (Notice the circumstance is the same because it is neutral and objectively true. I'm just going to choose a different thought about it.)

Thought (I could choose any one of these thoughts): (1) I don't want to write the memo, but I'm going to write it anyway. (2) I know I can do an amazing job writing this memo. (3) I can't wait to complete this memo so it's off my mind.

Feeling I feel confident.

Action I schedule an appropriate amount of time and write the memo.

Result I write the memo, I feel great about it, and it's off my mind!

It's that easy. When I'm lacking motivation, I can choose to think "I don't want to do this, and I'm going to do it anyway." It's similar to another one of my favorite mantras: *the only way out is through.* Our obstacles, fears, anxieties, and worries don't simply evaporate if we ignore the tasks and situations we don't want to face. If we can recognize that discomfort is only a feeling and that what we want lies on the other side of that feeling of discomfort, we can recognize that the only way out is through. We must do the thing we don't want to do. In completing the task at hand, the fear, anxiety, and trepidation involved dissipate.

Changing our thinking about the things we don't want to do makes all the difference.

When I can't get myself motivated, I choose to focus on the results I want, like getting a task off my mind/to-do list, celebrating completing that task (maybe with chips and guacamole), being proud of myself for getting it done, or reaping whatever rewards there are to reap from completing the task. Then I choose the thoughts, feelings, and actions that will get me that result. Rather than feeling afraid of the challenging, uncomfortable feelings that might come up when I'm doing the thing I don't want to do, I feel empowered to take whatever actions I need to take to get the results I want.

When uncomfortable feelings threaten to derail me or drain my motivation, I remind myself that I can do hard things. I'm not afraid of discomfort. Discomfort is just a feeling, and I can handle it. I can do the things I don't want to do, and by doing them I will get the results I want. Managing my mind helps me find the motivation I need.

KENDRA BRODIN, MSW, JD is the Founder and CEO of EsquireWell, providing innovative speaking, coaching, training, and online resources to accelerate lawyer well-being and success. She was formerly the Chief Attorney Development Officer at Taft, Stettinius & Hollister. In this role, Kendra managed firm-wide lawyer training and development as well as well-being initiatives. Kendra previously served as Director of Career and Professional Development at the University of St. Thomas School of Law, Manager of Business Development at an intellectual property law firm, Executive Director of a leading attorney search and staffing firm, and executive coach and consultant for lawyers and other professionals. Kendra is a frequent presenter on topics related to law student and lawyer career, professional, and personal development.

Kendra is a Past-President of Minnesota Women Lawyers and leads the Institute for Leadership in the Legal Profession signature program for the Hennepin County Bar Association. Kendra is on the Board of Directors of Lawyers Concerned for Lawyers (Minnesota) and is a member of the ABA Well-Being Committee and several other committees devoted to lawyer and law student well-being and professional development. Kendra is a certified coach and holds a certificate in Advanced Leadership Studies from the University of St. Catherine, a Masters degree in Social Work from the University of Pennsylvania, and a law degree from the University of Minnesota School of Law. Kendra lives in near St. Paul, Minnesota with her husband and three teenage children.

FULL CIRCLE FAITH: IT'S AN INSIDE JOB

by Kesha Kent

For the longest time, I wasn't being true to myself. But after a major shift in my life and mindset, I couldn't be more pleased with where I am today. I've come into alignment by doing the inside work, I've learned to bring my full authentic self into each and every space at every given moment. What a beautiful awakening! It's a daily task!

There was once a time in which code-switching was in full effect within me, along with some major people-pleasing. What is code-switching, you ask? Well, code-switching involves adjusting one's style of speech, appearance, behavior, and expression, in order to optimize the comfort of others in exchange for fair treatment, quality service, and employment opportunities. In my own words, code-switching is an internal desire to be included. It caused me to straighten my hair, adjust my mannerisms, and tune outward while minimizing my unique self. 1 required everyone's approval. Not anymore. I had a funeral for that old self, and now I'm watering all of the many seeds being planted in this current day!

I went back-and-forth for a few weeks really contemplating where I wanted to start with this writing process. I grappled with the concepts of manifestation and full-circle faith! These terms are so alive in my life today. My experiences are merely to motivate, inspire and remind you that each obstacle in life is designed to stretch us. Our words and mindset guide every move we make.

As I started this writing journey, I simply needed to breathe. Living through so much civil unrest, systemic racism and a pandemic as a woman of color is an exhausting feat, so I allowed myself a much-needed break. In this time of reflection, I took walks, went roller skating, pampered myself, danced, and even jumped double-dutch! All of these activities have helped me get back to the grounding I needed to be able to create. I now understand that taking care of myself is a must. With this newfound peace, I'm finally ready to come back to my story of FULL-CIRCLE FAITH!

A state of grounding has been key to my writing process, as this allows me to check in with myself! I'm so used to checking in with everyone but remembering myself has had to become an intentional act, and the results have been powerful. When I think about my full-circle faith, there have been so many instances in my life that come to mind. Join me on this journey.

In 2012, I was laid off, and things began to look dark for my family. We lost our home, we lost our cars, and most of all, we lost our dignity! During that time, the only thing that held our family together was faith, and as we look back today, each and everything we went through had purpose.

There was so much that quickly shifted during this time period. Our address changed, and our environment completely changed. Our family was so comfortable in our own space that staying with family members was uneasy! Still, I stood on my faith. I woke up every morning as if I were still heading to work. I took the bus to the local library after getting my children off to school. The staff at the library knew that I was looking for work and assisted me in the process. I enrolled in FREE Microsoft Office classes that were offered. I used the time to sharpen my skills. This gave me just another piece of confidence on my journey, having these FREE refresher classes were a gift. St. Louis Public Library was very integral in my healing journey as well.

I showed up to several interviews, many times taking public transportation to get there, enduring multiple two- to three-hour commutes, sometimes taking two buses to my interviews. I was determined! I met so many fascinating humans as I rode the Metrobus and Metrolink. I used the time to read and listen to audiobooks. Making the most of the situation was my decision, and looking back, I can recognize the purpose that time period served.

During this three-month period of being laid off, I was referred to Dress for Success to be suited in a professional suit for interviewing. I loved the experience so much that I started volunteering for the organization. This was my saving grace. I volunteered for roughly three weeks before landing a job offer with Ashley Furniture HomeStores. My new suit changed the game for me and elevated my confidence. My appearance in the suit spoke volumes, and I received a job offer on the spot at my second interview!

When I landed the job, I vowed to always refer other women to these services, and I did just that, and have continued doing so. Prior to finding Dress for Success, I had prayed constantly, asking God to connect me to resources! That's exactly what happened, and it has not stopped. Dress for Success has been a major part of my life. The sustainability, tools and confidence provided by the experience through resources and support were a critical part of how I was able to say 'yes' to myself.

My life changed forever in November 2018 when I said 'yes' to myself in a whole new way! At the time, I was working in a role I knew I was no longer able to serve in. The environment was toxic, which caused every area in my life to be off-balance. I was so good at people-pleasing, constantly making sure everyone around me had what they needed without asking myself if I had what I needed! I felt the effects of this behavior in every area in my life.

Looking back, the discomfort I was facing was a beautiful process of coming out of my cocoon and shutting off the valve of people pleasing! At that very moment, I spoke my truth out loud for the first time: I wanted to walk with purpose, fulfillment and joy! I had no idea what that meant; all I knew was that it was imperative for me to have joy in my work, which was missing.

I took a weeklong vacation to gain clarity and unplug from everything around me. I sat down and started envisioning what I wanted. I reflected on how I could show up authentically, loving my career and feeling valued. I didn't think that was too much to ask for.

Sadly, I knew for a little over a year that I was no longer fulfilled in the environment I was in, but I stayed complacent! It was time for change, so I returned from my vacation and immediately put in my two-week notice. I didn't have another opportunity lined up, nor a large book of business as an entrepreneur! What I clearly did have was myself, my faith, and the God-given gifts that were present within me.

As 2019 rolled around, I started out as a free agent and full-time entrepreneur! Those next six months were the best time of my life. I was able to slow down and completely reevaluate who I was. Having this break helped me declutter from the many years of being in toxic environments and suppressing my gifts and talents. I shut down the chatter each and every time it reared its ugly head. This time was truly a gift as I look back. Without completely revamping my heart and mind, I'd STILL be stuck in a rut of the unfulfilled rat race. It's in that YES that I begin to soar again!

Listen, if someone would've told me early on in my life that I possessed the power to decide my destiny, I would've started watching my words and my actions much sooner! But the truth is, it all happened exactly when it was supposed to. Let me take you on a journey of saying YES to me, to my creative genius, to my zone, and to all of my Kesha-ness.

During this time of internal reconciliation, I turned inward and found that every single thing that I believed about myself was in question. The people that were used to me allowing them to overflow my plate were in awe. Hell, I was in awe of myself. I've been able to land the career of my dreams as a Diversity Talent Specialist. I'm a new author, podcast host and talk show host. These things only happened because I promised to say yes to Kesha and say no to all the things that have attempted to remove the power I possess. This process has been an ongoing journey of self-care, prayer, meditation and removing doubt. I've used some amazing tools to help; *The Untethered Soul,* written by Michael A. Singer, and *The Four Agreements,* written by Don Miguel Ruiz. I constantly go back to these books on a weekly basis, sometimes even daily!

Despite what it looks or feels like, each step is ordered, and everything that is supposed to be WILL. I'm forever grateful for this journey of self-discovery and mastery, as it has changed the entire trajectory of my life, my legacy and all that I am creating.

I've been recently named one of five Global Ambassadors for Dress for Success. This opportunity will allow me to grow leaps and bounds through coaching, branding, and global media exposure. I'm one hundred percent sure this landed in my lap due to me saying YES to Kesha; I prayed for this. I'm so grateful for the journey!

KESHA KENT, CEO and Founder of MrsKeshSpeaks, is a wife, mother, a High Energy Speaker, Best Selling Author, Podcast Host and Diversity & Inclusion Leader with Ascension Healthcare.

She has over twenty years of Human Resources, Recruitment/agency staffing and Training and Development experience in healthcare, IT, and sales industry!

Mrs. Kent holds a Bachelor's degree in Management and Leadership and a Master's degree in Organizational Leadership both from Judson University in Elgin, Illinois.

She's the new author of Amazon's #1 new release *Networking, It's Your SuperPower!,* released Juneteenth 2020 and new podcast *Networking, It's Your SuperPower!*

A "MINDFUL MINDSET" APPROACH: MY PATH TO FINDING INNER PEACE

by Roslyn (Roz) M. Pitts

"The peace you want is already in you, you just can't feel it because the mind is making too much noise." – Eckhart Tolle

Tolle's quote resonated with me the second I read it. For a long time, my mind was NOISY and filled with loud, distracting, and sometimes unpleasant thoughts. There was a constant loop in my head that repeated statements like: *you're just not quite good enough, you're always a step behind, you'll never reach your goals,* and *no one wants to hear what you have to say.*

Even worse than walking around with a head full of disparaging thoughts was the fact that I often believed them. I could write a list as long as this page of events in which I didn't reach my goals and "perceived" that I had outright failed. My self-attributed defeats weren't uncommon, and some could rightfully say that my defeats were a walk in the park compared to the burdens carried by others. But they were mine nonetheless, and they often felt heavy.

Though I carried this negativity with me throughout my life, there was always a positive force inside of me that was in constant conflict with my negative side. Surprisingly enough, one of my core traits and values is positivity. Positivity even comes up as my number one strength on the Clifton Strengths Personality Assessment! I've always been a glass-half-full type person in the eyes of friends and family, who see me as someone who laughs heartily and sees beauty and joy in situations that others may not.

I'm not sure what it was that opened me up to the "new perspective" exercise employed by an executive coach I met two years ago...and it may not really matter. Maybe I unconsciously grew tired of the dissonance between the noise in my mind and the lightness in my heart. During that "life-adjusting" coaching session, I described the disappointments throughout my life – the long list of events in which I didn't reach my goals and perceived that I had failed. My executive coach invited me to take a different perspective. She asked that I look at my goals from a place of accomplishment, rather than failure. Like a new pair of glasses, that new lens allowed me to see victories where I couldn't see them before. My black-and-white view of the world instantly turned into a multi-colored rainbow of possibilities!

I can point to that exact exercise, that very moment, as the time when I first opened up to the possibility that my assumptions and notions about my failures only represented one perspective, and wasn't the entire truth. Finally seeing the noise in my head as no more than destructive chatter was perhaps my closest experience of true "enlightenment."

This was a step, maybe even a leap, in the right direction! But this clarity did not solve the essential problem in front of me: how to quiet the noise within and achieve true inner peace. My approach was unfamiliar and had to evolve over time but looking back it now makes perfect sense.

My journey began with the practice of true mindfulness through the study of Buddhist teachings, meditation and yoga. These practices led me down the path of gratitude, which helped me to discover my desire to embrace all the positive moments in life. As I developed mindfulness and gratitude practices, I ultimately turned to a lessor travelled path – the path to inner peace.

THE MINDFUL PATH

Shortly after my father died, I searched for ways to manage my grief. Like many others, I took a not so unusual path and turned to yoga in the midst of my struggle.

I didn't immediately fall in love with the practice as so many do, however. My body was unfamiliar with the poses, and my mind resisted the need to slow down. However, over time, I magically discovered the beauty and benefits of a healthy yoga practice. Once I became familiar with the poses, my body moved almost instinctively.

But more importantly, my mind had the space to observe my thoughts, which proved both frightening and liberating at the same time. At first my thoughts raced like dogs in a fox hunt, but eventually they floated like cumulous clouds in a pale blue sky.

I've spent many inspiring hours in a multitude of different yoga and meditation studios, completed two 200-hour yoga teacher training courses, embraced meditation as a tool to calm the mind and soul, and studied Buddhist teachings. To this day, all of these practices speak to me and align with the values that I aspire to live my life by.

THE GRATEFUL PATH

As I travelled my mindful path, the practice of gratitude became a common theme. Despite the challenges of life, I realized that there is so much to be grateful for. Over time, I learned that thinking more intentionally about the role of gratitude brought me sustained joy.

Not surprisingly, gratitude positively impacts our brains. Research links gratitude to major health benefits such as strengthening the immune system and reducing inflammation, improving sleep quality, increasing feelings of optimism, reducing stress and depression, and ultimately increasing social inclusion.[*]

We typically feel gratitude when a benefit has been given to us unexpectedly. This could be a joyful emotion, time with a dear friend, the beauty of nature or the taste of a delicious family recipe.

But there are many ways to raise awareness of gratitude, rather than waiting for it to arise. Some methods include journaling, tuning into the present moment through meditation, creating a gratitude jar, or writing a thank you note.

[*] The Mindful Staff, "How to Practice Gratitude," *Mindful*, November 26, 2020 www.mindful.org/an-introduction-to-mindful-gratitude.

For me, I practice gratitude by simply noticing the things throughout my day that happen without much effort – trees dancing in the wind, cats jumping like jack rabbits, or friends greeting each other with bear hugs. I've found that even during the most challenging of times, I can find moments of gratitude. Believe me, they are always there.

THE PEACEFUL PATH

What is inner peace, really? While everyone has a unique definition, for me inner peace is about living a fulfilled, joyful life that aligns with my values, and surrounding myself with people who share those values. I also associate inner peace with slowing down, calmness, balance, wellbeing, and living a simpler life.

As with any goal, it is ideal to have a clear vision of the ultimate destination. But in the case of inner peace, this is nearly impossible.

There isn't a playbook for inner peace, and the search will likely be very different for you than for me. I started my journey with meditation and a focus on self-reflection, as I worked to marry my thoughts, personal beliefs and core values with my daily intentions and actions.

Ultimately, my practice helped me uncover that I have unreasonably high expectations for myself. Too often, I focus on future outcomes *(I'll be happy "when" I graduate from law school, when I find the perfect job, when I get married, when I retire)*. Too often, I launched into an impossible battle with elements of life that are out of my control. This realization helped me understand that living in the present moment and addressing the things that I can change is a more productive use of my energy.

Unfortunately, the journey towards inner peace requires difficult decisions, and the courage to identify, confront and eliminate negative forces that often appear as demons or saboteurs. Some decisions are easier than others, but most of them take time and require uncomfortable self-reflection.

The hardest part for me has been recognizing the things that no longer serve me, finding the strength and willingness to step away from them, and venturing into the "healthy" unknown. For example, exploring new job opportunities after committing seventeen years to the same law firm, or unexpectedly deciding to move away from family and friends to a new city in search of new life experiences and adventures.

Perhaps the most difficult decisions, however, are those we face involving toxic situations or people whose values and outlooks are dramatically different from ours. I've let go of close friends with whom I previously enjoyed many shared interests, as I began to notice subtle clues indicating that their views on social justice, equality and human rights-related issues do not align with my values. Because their views stood in conflict with my core values, I knew I could no longer maintain the relationship in the same way.

I've learned to observe and trust my intuition. If something is a constant source of frustration, worry or grief, I proactively explore the reasons why. From there, I decide whether, and how, change can occur. This approach takes time, as soul searching rarely uncovers a crystal-clear path. However, because I strive to be present, observe my thoughts, and trust my decisions, I find myself on my never-ending path to inner peace during all phases of my life.

IN CLOSING

We live in a world of chaos, confusion and difficulties, but life is also beautiful, magical and filled with endless possibilities. There is no such thing as a 'perfect' life, and everyone faces challenges along the way. I recognize that I am extremely fortunate and have so much to be grateful for, and it has been easier for me to deal with life's challenges through mindfulness and gratitude practices. These practices have led me to a more positive and satisfying life. Ultimately, my most important goal is my continual advancement towards lasting inner peace.

ROSLYN (ROZ) M. PITTS is the Director of Professional Development and Well-Being at Katten. She started her professional career as an environmental lawyer. After seven years of practice, she discovered her passion for talent and built a career focusing on legal talent management strategies: attorney recruitment, training, development, engagement and retention, orientation and integration, coaching, mentoring, performance management, and well-being.

Roz received her J.D. from the Dickinson School of Law and BA in International Relations with a minor in Economics from Boston University. She is also a Certified Lawyer Coach, Mental Health First Aid First Responder and certified yoga instructor. Roz lives just outside of Asheville, North Carolina, with her husband, Eric Dickerson, and two cats. She enjoys playing pickle ball, golfing and mountain living.

STRENGTHENING YOUR WORKDAY MINDSET

by Drew Amoroso

I n 2015, I was four years into a career as a lawyer at a prominent US law firm.

Though my firm was fantastic and I felt fortunate to have started my career around such thoughtful and supportive colleagues, I felt like I had a different professional purpose to pursue.

That summer, I went on a vacation and did something I had never done before: I turned off my phone for three days straight. I spent my time reading books and just sitting with my thoughts about the future.

That three-day stretch gave me a sense of energy and clarity that I'd never experienced before. It helped shift my attention toward uncovering my 'why' and my professional path.

Looking back, I realized that my most rewarding moments were when I was helping other professionals learn the power of a healthy mindset, sharing how this could improve their workday and allow them to develop into their best professional self.

I eventually left my big law job and founded a coaching startup that helped train lawyers. The company has since grown into a technology startup that connects lawyers with coaches in the legal industry who provide professional development coaching.

The decision to leave my career in law was a challenging transformation. I transitioned from a nice, safe, secure position with a clear trajectory to an entrepreneurial path that felt fraught with uncertainty, at least initially.

In those early days of building my startup, I woke up many mornings with a pit in my stomach and a head filled with disempowering thoughts.

I don't have what it takes to build this company. No one's going to see my vision or want my help. There's nothing special about what I'm creating. This isn't going to work.

These beliefs churned beneath the surface for many months as I tried to follow my vision and design a new way of living.

At one point, about nine months in, I remember having a realization: at the root of every challenge I faced was an originating thought, feeling or emotion, in connection with that challenge.

In other words, if I went behind the "challenge" itself and dug down to its origin, I would find that the challenge was ultimately grounded in how I was *thinking* about that external experience.

When I was feeling stressed because things weren't moving quickly enough, that stress originated from a thought about the work.

When I felt anxious about whether a client would say yes to a proposal, that anxiousness originated from a thought or belief I had about what that client was going to say in response to the proposal.

Realizing that a limiting belief or an old way of thinking was at the heart of every one of my challenges led me to see that the *solution* to every one of my challenges began with a new originating thought.

In order to change my day-to-day experience, I had to first commit to a shift in the way I was thinking, at the root level.

The challenges I faced in building my startup had very little to do with the work itself, and everything to do with how I was thinking about the work.

This series of realizations got me thinking even more about the power of mindset and how a fundamental shift in perception is at the heart of any change we want to see.

My interest in mindset blossomed into writing, speaking, and developing courses focused on what I eventually called Workday Mindset.

At a high level, Workday Mindset is the set of beliefs and attitudes you use to shape your thought processes and respond to situations at work.

If you think about it, every workday is comprised of dozens of mini-situations that we each have to think through: processing the actions of colleagues and clients, managing stressors and emotions, pursuing opportunities, and navigating challenging situations, along with many other situations that you have to think through to determine how you're going to respond.

It turns out that the way we move through a workday is influenced by the way we think through these situations, not the presence of the situations themselves.

Of course, other people and things that happen around us have the potential to influence our thoughts. But at the end of the day, it's really the way that we think about the situations that determines how we respond.

I like to think about your Workday Mindset as a filter. Everything that happens around you, and all of the inputs you have to manage, get put through a filter that you have designed based on the way you want to perceive your workday.

You get to decide how you want to respond to situations, engage with people, handle opportunities, and ultimately shape the kind of day-to-day experiences you want to create for yourself.

Strengthening your Workday Mindset can be challenging because we've been conditioned to view our workdays through the lens of what we can control. When something is out of our control, that's when we start to feel powerless, which leads to emotions and thoughts that do not serve us.

Even if we don't always have the ability to directly influence what happens to us or around us, one thing we always have the ability to influence is the way we *think* and respond to those things. We always get to decide. That's the beauty of a strong Workday Mindset.

Importantly, if we don't set up the parameters for how we want to think throughout our day, then our mind is ripe for letting in any thought that wants to get in, whether it's a helpful thought or not. Fear, worry, limiting beliefs and other disempowering thoughts will occupy that space by default in an effort to protect us and keep us safe.

In response, we can create a framework that allows us to have an intentional, consistent approach to monitoring and shaping the way we think. With a framework, we can gently train our mind to have a different response to situations, thoughts, feelings or emotions that get in the way of us showing up at our best.

In my opinion, this is the most important thing we can do for ourselves in a workday because it influences everything else that we do. If we want to change our experience, we must first change the state of our mindset.

There are many Workday Mindset concepts that can be used to help design our new way of thinking. The most impactful one I've relied on over the years is one my dad taught me related to situational awareness.

In the workday context, situational awareness is your ability to be present and recognize an opportunity to think or act with intention in the moment.

Rather than simply reacting to something, this means having the presence of mind to acknowledge that you're in a challenging situation where you can deploy a type of thinking that will help you navigate through that moment.

One way to hone your situational awareness is to practice a concept called First Thought, Second Thought, First Action.

Here's how it works.

It's hard to influence the first thought that pops into your mind. For example, if I were to tell you to not think of a big yellow dump truck, it's nearly impossible not to picture one immediately. We can't really prevent that first thought from entering our mind.

We generally do, however, have the ability to influence our second thought and the first action we decide to take thereafter. So, while we might not be able to change our immediate thought about a situation we encounter, we do have the ability to influence what happens next.

Here's an example from my own professional experience. One situation that always resulted in a stressful reaction for me was when I received constructive feedback. When someone would tell me that they disagreed with me or made significant revisions to my work, it felt like a personal attack. I equated feedback with the belief that the feedback provider didn't think my work was good enough, and that it was only a matter of time before they realized that I had no idea what I was doing.

If you find yourself having a reactionary first thought like this in response to a stressful situation, that's okay. The idea here is to catch yourself having that thought and replace it with a constructive second thought that suits you better.

Your second thought, for example, might be something like this: *the feedback I receive is not a commentary on me as a person; it's actually a vehicle the feedback provider is using to make our work together even better and provide me with a chance to learn. It's a golden opportunity to improve, and I'm thankful that they brought this to my attention.*

With that second thought in place, you can then go about taking your first action with intentionality and perspective. In my example, that action might be to incorporate the feedback with an understanding that it's actually for everyone's highest good. Thinking about feedback in this way helps to shrink the intensity and frequency of a reactive first thought, changing it from a negative to a positive.

This is just one example of the power of Workday Mindset. Building a framework with intention – and running your thoughts through it like a filter – helps you realize that even though your day may be filled with thoughts that aren't suiting you, you do have the ability to gently, and over time, change the way you think.

DREW AMOROSO is the founder of DueCourse, a platform that connects lawyers and law firms with personal, professional, and business development coaches.

He started his career as a lawyer and now trains professionals across the country on how to strengthen their mindset and design their workday.

He's the host of *The Workday Mindset Podcast* and an adjunct professor at several Bay Area law schools where he teaches a Practice Ready Seminar, a course that helps students design their career with intention.

SILENCE, SLEDGEHAMMER, AND SELF-PITY: HOW I DISCOVERED THE PATH TO HAPPINESS

by Yuliya LaRoe

T he idea to attend a Vipassana meditation course came to me as all wild things do – at a party. Among the casual and comfortable cheerfulness, I randomly overheard a group of people behind me having a conversation about one of their friends, who had just returned from a ten-day silent retreat in Northern California.

Ten days in complete silence; say what?! As a former lawyer, that sounded absolutely *insane* to me, and something that I felt I absolutely must do. All right, Vipassana – here I come!

WHO WANTS TO GET ENLIGHTENED? I DO!

On the day I arrived at the Vipassana meditation center, we were all ushered into the dining room and given some basic instructions: keep noble silence (no verbal, physical, or visual contact of any kind), refrain from any contact with the opposite sex (men and women are separated for the entire duration of the course), and maintain a strict adherence to the course schedule, which required us to wake up at four o'clock in the morning and meditate for over ten hours per day.

Before I continue, I guess it's time to come clean. When I arrived, I fully intended to "get enlightened" during my meditation experience. Yep, full-on enlightenment... nothing else would do.

Looking back, I realize how silly that sounds. I mean, who actually gets "enlightened"? But that was pretty much how I approached life in general: all or nothing, black or white, right or wrong. I had high expectations for myself in everything I did and didn't tolerate failure of any kind. I would beat myself up for not meeting my own expectations and judge myself harshly for every failure, whether real or perceived. Type-A overachiever, you say? Yep, that sounds about right.

The first day of the retreat started out pretty rough. I overslept! I woke up at the sound of my alarm at 4 a.m., as I was supposed to, but quickly decided that getting up at such an ungodly hour was just ridiculous. Suddenly, it was 5:30 a.m. The birds were chirping, the sun had started to come up, and I was totally late. Well done! I got ready as quickly as I could, rushed to the meditation hall, and sat out a pretty torturous hour, counting the minutes until the gong would sound, announcing breakfast. *Oh, dear God, what have I gotten myself into?* From that point on, it got a lot worse before it got better...

Days one through three are frankly a total blur. I got up every morning at 4:20 a.m. and meditated for hours throughout the day. Pure torture.

Most of my meditations in those first few days went something like this:

> "Alright, let's meditate! So pumped for it. I can tell I'll do really well today. Ok, inhale, exhale... So, I wonder what's for lunch today... I hope something yummy... And wow, it's freezing here! I really didn't need to pack all these t-shirts... Ouch, my neck (back, knee, etc.) hurts... Shuffle, shuffle... Still not comfortable... Ugh... Gotta get some more cushions... Ha, I think the woman next to me fell asleep and just woke herself up with a snore... Ha ha ha ha... Oh no! I am supposed to be observing my breath! Okay, alright... Inhale, exhale, inhale, exhale... Gotta call the store when I get back to LA to see if they can order that cute jacket I saw in my size... It's so pretty here – I love all the pine trees. Gorgeous! La-la-la, la-la-la, la-la-la... Oh, not again! I'm really lousy at this..."

It amazed me just how little control I had over my mind. After observing just one or two breaths, it was already wandering off. Frankly, I was shocked by the amount of useless stuff that kept flying into my head.

But after a while, I got the hang of it, and overall I felt like I was doing alright. But then came the fifth day.

EQUANIMITY IS THE NAME OF THE GAME

On day five, the facilitators explained that the next stage of the meditation process was to mentally observe each body part while noticing and acknowledging any sensations in that section of the body. The trick was that this surveying process had to be accomplished while remaining completely objective and equanimous regardless of whether the sensations experienced were pleasant, unpleasant or non-existent. By constantly keeping the mind focused on the present moment, the meditator could gain experiential insight, realizing that none of the feelings were permanent and that feelings of attachment or aversion to the sensation (the cause of all misery) were useless, as these sensations (just like anything else in the world) would eventually and inevitably disappear.

This made sense, and I felt ready to nail this next stage! But halfway through the day I started to feel irritation creep up, and thoughts of frustration and panic began to slowly overtake my mind.

> *"Ugh, I am making such slow progress. I am probably not even doing it right. What if I never get it right? All these people around me will get all enlightened, and I'll be the only unenlightened loser…".*

No matter how hard I tried to calm myself down or move away from these thoughts, they persisted.

Then the irritation started to grow into a full-blown rage, something I do not experience often. My mind decided that, rather than meditating, it wanted to focus on the noises in the room.

> *"Oh God, the sounds coming from the stomach of the woman sitting next to me are SO ANNOYING! What the hell did she eat today? I mean, honestly, what's going on in there? It's like she is digesting an elephant. And HOW IRRITATING is the guy across the room, who keeps swallowing all the time… it's like every twenty seconds… What's the problem, buddy? Stop thinking about food and focus! This is so distracting and frustrating! I am really trying my best here, but these people are just not letting me focus. I swear, one more sound from this woman or one more swallow from that guy and I will have to say something!"*

My level of irritation, annoyance and anger was rising so rapidly that at some point I started seeing visions of smashing these people's heads with a sledgehammer (!!!). I could not believe that I, typically so mild-mannered and proper, was having these violent thoughts. The feelings of self-pity and judgment completely overtook me, and I felt tears run down my face. "Oh, now this is just perfect. You are going to cry in public and show everyone what a loser you are?!?! Well done. Really, well done!"

Of course, no one but me cared about this, as each person was most likely going through their own personal mental drama. Another significant contributing factor to my state of temporary insanity was the fact that, on day five, our group meditation sittings (each one hour long, three times a day) became the Sittings of Strong Determination, which meant that we couldn't move or change our position for the entire duration of the meditation. This, of course, caused all sorts of physical pain and discomfort.

By the end of the fifth day, I felt like I'd been through a meat grinder. I was completely exhausted, physically and mentally, and no longer cared if I was doing it right or if others could see my internal struggles (which actually felt good). I realized that once I let go of my attachment to doing it right, being perfect, achieving a quick result, and judging myself, I felt free to focus on the actual process and not worry about the ultimate outcome. Sure enough (and not surprisingly, really) my meditation began to flow more smoothly, the sounds in the room no longer bothered me, and I was able to endure the Sittings of Strong Determination with more ease.

That was my turning point. While my meditations did not become effortless after this, my mental state and my attitude towards the meditation process had changed completely, which in turn transformed my entire experience.

Prior to this experience, I had often heard that we create our reality through our own perception of what is actually going on, through our interpretations of the factual reality. This, however, was the first time I actually experienced it to be true, and what an amazing insight it was: I get to choose how I feel about something (whether it's pleasant or not), and, thus, I am one hundred percent responsible for, and in control of, the quality of my life! How beautifully simple and obvious…

NO, I DID NOT REACH ENLIGHTENMENT, BUT…

So, what did I learn from those ten days? To start with the obvious, a powerful meditation technique. What else? Well, that:

- true wisdom can come only from within following a personal experience. While intellectual understanding is a useful and necessary tool, it results in knowledge, not wisdom;
- our lives are governed by the law of impermanence. Nothing ever stays the same – all is created to pass away. Everything is in a constant flux and flow. We are born to (live, but ultimately to) die. With every passing minute, we are one minute closer to our death. This is the law of nature, and neither science nor magic can change that. But we get to decide how we are going to spend these minutes, hours, days, months, years; and
- to realize true happiness and experience pure joy in our day-to-day lives, we must learn to accept each moment as it is and stop fighting it or trying to turn it into something else.

Things I've lost? A couple of pounds, some sleep, and hopefully, a few layers of the ego and the old self-destructing reactionary habit patterns of the wild "monkey mind."*

* According to Buddhist principles, the "monkey mind" is a term that refers to being unsettled, restless, or confused.

HOW I USE MY INSIGHTS TODAY

This experience, more than anything else I've done, has helped me to become more patient and resilient. They say that running one's own business is a "full-contact sport." It's true! There is a lot of uncertainty. Some plans take a lot longer to work out than anticipated. Some things don't work out at all.

In the past, I would get frustrated and get down on myself when things didn't go according to plan. When contacts didn't reply to my outreach. When a client didn't re-engage my company for more work, or when a new program didn't get traction.

I would spend so much time ruminating about why things happened the way they did, but, when things did go according to plan, I would take it as a given. But why? Nothing is guaranteed to us!

Now I approach things differently. I remind myself daily that both my successes and my failures, the good and the bad, are here only temporarily. And this one thought allows me to focus on the positive without getting too attached to it, and to work through the frustrating patches without getting too bogged down in them. They too shall pass.

Interestingly, I am just as passionate about my work as I ever was, just with a lot less anxiety and a lot more ease.

YULIYA LAROE, JD, PCC, ELI-MP

For over a decade, Yuliya LaRoe has partnered with leaders and organizations who believe, as she does, that business and professional growth is directly tied to personal growth. An experienced ICF-credentialed executive and business coach and the founder of LeadWise Group (leadwisegroup.com), Yuliya helps professionals increase their leadership and business effectiveness, including coaching lawyers on how to secure high level corporate clients. Over the last ten years, Yuliya coached and trained hundreds of lawyers to achieve tangible business development results, such as growing client billings from $100,000 to over $1,000,000 annually, signing on new high profile clients, achieving equity partnership status, and much more.

Prior to coaching leaders and lawyers, Yuliya served as legal counsel and advisor to Fortune 500 companies on a variety of issues related to their global operations.

After growing up in Russia, Yuliya spent fifteen years in Southern California. She now calls Miami her home, where she resides with her husband and a brood of mischievous pets. Yuliya is an avid international traveler and is passionate about personal development and inner growth. Something few people know about Yuliya is that in one year she spent two months volunteering in Costa Rica, traveled to South Korea and Russia, completed a four-month yoga teacher certification course, backpacked around India for a month, and attended a ten-day silent meditation retreat!

FORGIVING YOUR WAY THROUGH OBSTACLES IN THE WORKPLACE

by Rocky Galloway

I pride myself on doing an excellent job – not just a good job, but an excellent job. My personal brand is based on excellence and integrity; it is who I am and who I like to believe I have always been. It is something in which I find great pride and satisfaction, so it is especially hard when any aspect of my brand is called into question.

Several years ago, after spending many years with a Fortune 100 company, I found myself in the unique position of qualifying for an early retirement package. I could have played it safe (as safe as anything is in Corporate America) and stayed with the company, but after thinking it through carefully and weighing all the pros and cons, I elected to take the package. It was so great to have time to think critically about the next phase of my career. I began a very intentional journey to find a new and exciting opportunity that fit my skills, talents and interests.

As exhilarating as that time was, it was also sobering and self-reflective. I soon came to the recognition that if it had not been for the early retirement offer, I probably wouldn't have taken it upon myself to initiate a job search. Although I had many challenging and fulfilling roles during my career at the company, once that chapter ended, I realized that I had allowed myself to become very comfortable there. Perhaps too comfortable.

As a consequence, my search took on added emphasis and intentionality. I forced myself to stretch and consider roles that did not necessarily fit the pure job descriptions of my previous positions. That led to the development of a functional resume focused on skills that could be transferable to multiple opportunities. The second part of that equation was conveying my newly identified transferable skills to recruiters and hiring managers, encouraging them to think outside the box, which was not always easy.

Soon, an interesting opportunity came to my attention. It was a chance to take my experience as in-house counsel to a large IT systems integrator and use it to benefit a medium-sized company in a totally different field – telecommunications. For me, it was a full circle moment. After undergraduate school, I started my career in telecommunications and worked in the field immediately prior to starting law school. I was very excited about the prospect of this new job. After several interviews, I was hired and embarked upon the next chapter of my career.

As with any new job, there is a learning curve associated with the responsibilities of the position, the organizational structure, corporate processes/procedures, and the people. I approached the learning enthusiastically, looking for ways to add immediate value in my new role. Unfortunately, it soon became apparent that one component of the learning – people – would challenge me in ways that I had never been challenged in the two decades of my professional career before that.

Within six months on the job, I learned that I was being characterized in ways that had nothing to do with who I was or had ever been in the workplace. It forced me to reflect upon whether I was somehow showing up at this new position differently than I had shown up at any position in the past.

It all began on a Friday afternoon during a call with my manager, which I initially took to be a routine check-in call. I could not have been more mistaken. My manager proceeded to inform me that I was creating a disruption in the office and that "it had to stop." To say I was completely blindsided is an understatement. In fact, it was so absurd that I honestly thought she was joking and asked if she was serious. She informed me that this was indeed a very serious matter and that if the behavior did not cease, it would be reflected in my performance evaluation and could lead to termination. Among other things, I was told that I was not a team player, that I worked to undermine my colleagues, and that I had no respect for the chain of command in my organization. I listened intently and started taking notes. I asked for specific examples of the behavior and for the source of the information (which she could not have personal knowledge of given that her office was located over 1,000 miles and two time zones away). She refused to give me any of the information I requested.

I left that call feeling stunned. It felt like I had somehow been transported into an alternate universe. I had just completed a call with my manager telling me about behavior that could not be further from who I am as a professional and as a person.

I took some time to reflect on the conversation and jotted down more notes to make sure I captured all the events accurately. I then went to the office of a trusted colleague and shared the conversation I'd just had with our manager. I asked for his honest assessment of whether any of the characterizations attributed to me were accurate based on his observations of me in the workplace. He said they were not and seemed genuinely surprised that this was the feedback I received.

The weekend after the call was a blur – I literally did not sleep for the next two nights. Each time I tried to close my eyes, I kept replaying past interactions with my colleagues and clients in my mind, wondering if that was the situation that caused me to receive such negative feedback. *"Could it be this? No, it couldn't be that. Maybe it was this other situation."* Ultimately, I came up with nothing except exhaustion.

One of the questions I had to wrestle with was whether it was possible that I was somehow showing up differently in this new position than I had at other positions in the past. I also wondered whether my view of myself in the workplace was entirely wrong and that maybe I had been perceived in a negative light in other positions as well. In my heart, I did not think so, but in my quest to make sense of these bizarre set of circumstances, I had to allow for that possibility, so I reached out to colleagues that I worked closely with over the past fifteen plus years. None of them described me in the way I had been characterized.

There was another aspect of this experience that I had to face as well. Given that my manager had no firsthand knowledge of my interactions in the workplace because of her remote office location, it was likely that someone I worked with had provided her with this information. Someone she respected and trusted enough to believe the information conveyed without question, providing her with the confidence to confront me about it as if it were factual. This likely meant that it was someone I worked with closely, perhaps even another colleague. It also meant that my manager had not taken the time to truly get to know me. If she had, I believe she would have questioned the information and its veracity. Then even if she decided to have a conversation with me about it, the approach would have been "This is the feedback I have received, let's talk about it" rather than establishing the veracity of the information without any conversation with me beforehand. This was perhaps the most hurtful part. Frankly, as I reflect on it now, it was also a major failure on her part as a manager.

After that weekend of self-reflection and many, many conversations with colleagues past and present, I wrote a rebuttal to my manager, respectfully disagreeing with her assessment and asking for another conversation where we could go deeper into the reasons for her assessment and discuss any corrective actions. That conversation eventually happened and though I did not gain any additional source information, my manager retracted the threats of termination and performance improvement plans.

In the aftermath of all that I have described, I was left to do my work in an environment where basic trust had been broken. I did not know who to trust. I felt I had to watch my every step and every interaction for fear that it might be misinterpreted and play into the narrative that I was a disruptive force in the workplace and not a team player. I considered leaving but I truly enjoyed the work. In hindsight, I see how being in that situation was not conducive to me bringing my full self to the work. I second-guessed decisions and spent way too much time rewriting emails and other correspondence to make sure that the tone was proper and could not be misinterpreted. It was exhausting and very demoralizing.

Unfortunately, this went on for many months. Even though no actions were taken against me by my manager and my job seemed secure, the hurt and distrust remained. It began to impair my effectiveness at work, which was inconsistent with my personal brand of excellence. I desperately needed a change, a shift in perception, if I were to stay in the job and be a valuable contributor. It became clearer and clearer that I was holding on to the hurt and distrust to my own detriment. The catalyst for my then-current situation had long passed. Now I was hurting myself, and it was up to me to change that.

So, what changed? In a word, Forgiveness. As hokey and trite as it may sound, the practice of forgiveness was my path through. I set an intention to actively forgive everyone who may have been involved in the circumstances that led to that Friday afternoon telephone call, including my manager and colleagues. I simply forgave and let it all go. That act of forgiveness created the shift in mindset that was necessary to open new opportunities for how I might operate in my chosen workplace. Rather than continually asking "Why me?", I came to a level of radical acceptance that "This really happened to me." My mindset shifted from one of "Distrust" to "Trust but Verify." Lastly, I shifted from "Hurt and Withdrawal" to "Full Engagement." Of course, none of this happened overnight. However, when I look back on it, it was remarkable how quickly things began to change.

I began to settle back into who I am (my values, my talents, my gifts) and with that I slowly began to step more fully back into the work. I was more engaged, my solutions were more creative and my advice more grounded in the needs of the business. I took risks that I would not have been comfortable taking before. I soon began to receive recognition for my work from my colleagues and the teams I supported. That recognition was then reflected in my performance evaluations and compensation awards, which were some of the best I had received in my career up to that point.

Today, I still don't know the genesis of the perception that led to that Friday afternoon conversation with my manager. Truthfully, it no longer matters. What matters is the process which led to the shift in mindset that created a new reality for me. And for that, I will be forever grateful.

ROCKY GALLOWAY is an attorney and business leader with over twenty years of experience working in law firm and corporate environments supporting private sector and government clients. He is widely recognized for his ability to create successful business outcomes through strategic partnerships and creative solutions that benefit clients and their customers.

Outside of his professional pursuits, Rocky volunteers his time to benefit local community-based organizations through pro bono legal services and mentoring programs. Rocky and his family currently reside in the Washington DC metropolitan area.

Rocky holds a law degree from Howard University School of Law and a Bachelor of Science Degree in electrical engineering, also from Howard University. He is a Fellow of the Emerging Leaders Program, U.S. – Southern Africa Center for Leadership and Public Values.

PICK ME! THE WANING WISDOM OF WAITING FOR OTHERS TO RECOGNIZE MY WORTH

by Neha Sampat

I used to think that I needed to wait for people to recognize me. I believed I had to wait for people to acknowledge my expertise and to figure out for themselves who I was and what I could do. I was conditioned to hold these beliefs, both as a woman and as a person of color. I had been implicitly taught that I wasn't allowed to carve out my space. Rather, I was to speak when spoken to and wait to be called upon. In retrospect, I realize that this kept me from really stepping into who I was and the unique impact I could have on the world around me.

When I started my own business, it was just me. I built my company from the ground up. I remember feeling tentative about calling myself "CEO" because it felt too big for me, and I worried that I was too small for such a title. So I settled on calling myself "founder," almost with an invisible question mark after it, asking others to confirm whether or not I deserved that title, whether I was a legit entrepreneur, and whether I actually had any expertise to offer. For too long, I was uncomfortable saying what I was good at, because it felt like bragging. I felt like I was making a bigger deal of myself than I should. I didn't want others to think negatively of me for speaking about what I was good at.

But as I started my business, I had a real problem: If I wasn't talking about my company's services, what I was good at, and how I could help people, how was anyone ever going to hire me? This led me to begin exploring my own perceptions and how they had been shaped. I started to wonder if, by not owning my expertise and not speaking my name, I was perhaps making a *smaller* deal of myself than I should. Maybe my smallness was fiction, and maybe my expertise was fact!

As I was perusing my LinkedIn feed one day, I noticed a post about a large conference for women leaders at top companies. The person who made the post was looking to curate the program agenda, listing desired speaker qualifications and asking for recommendations. A big believer in promoting my fellow women, I immediately thought of a few uniquely impactful speakers in my circle who met the qualifications listed. I enthusiastically commented on the post and recommended them. As I scanned the other comments, I marveled at the caliber of speakers and leaders who were recommended, and I found myself wishing someone would recommend me. I glanced back at the list of qualifications and recognized that I easily met them all. I thought about how perfectly aligned my message about owning your value was with this opportunity. And I realized that I had one more recommendation I wanted to make: Myself!

Why was I waiting and wishing for someone else to type my name when I could just as easily type it myself? Why was I waiting for someone to recognize me among this caliber of speakers and leaders?

Well, because I knew that recommending myself could backfire in a number of ways. I could just imagine the original poster seeing my self-recommendation, rolling her eyes, and thinking, "Wow. Who does this Neha lady think she is?" I could imagine other people reading the post, thinking with pity as they read my comment, "No one else recommended her. She had to recommend herself. How sad!" Or maybe reading my comment with judgment: "How arrogant of her!"

I remembered reading a flurry of other posts and discussions on LinkedIn on the topic of whether one should call oneself an expert. Most who commented agreed that to do so was bad form and a bad look, as the label "expert" was to be bestowed upon you by others and was not yours for the taking. As I scanned through all the comments on those posts, I noticed with intrigue that the majority of people judging self-proclaimed experts as "frauds" were white men. I know now that, due to bias (oftentimes even unconscious), those in positions of power (still mostly white men) tend to sponsor, mentor, and promote those who remind them of themselves. So the system of bias works to define "expertise" in the model of white men, some of whom then claim the role as the arbiters of expertise, essentially saying, "Wait until *we* recognize your expertise before you call yourself an expert. Wait for us to speak your name." Trusting the system that I initially failed to recognize was flawed, I had spent too much of my life waiting for my worth to be recognized. I mean, this went way back!

I vividly remember my painful junior high years. As a nerdy brown girl from an immigrant family in a very white (and too-often racist) town, I was a social pariah. I was always picked last or almost last in gym class. It always stung, and every single time, I hoped that things would go differently.

I felt my flicker of hope fan into a flame on kickball day, as kickball was one game this nerdy brown girl was damn good at! Sadly, however, I was again picked last. "OK, fine," I thought, as I trudged over to my team. "They just forgot that I'm good at kickball."

And then the game began, and I did my thing. I exceeded even my own expectations by outplaying everyone, delivering a resounding and expertly-placed homerun kick to drive my team to victory!

The teacher blew her whistle and gathered us all at home plate to reshuffle the teams. She assigned a new pair of popular kids to pick new teams for the next game. I puffed myself up with confidence, daring to think, "This is it! Not only will I *not* be picked last, but I may even be picked *first!*" But no, I wasn't picked first. (Hmmm.) By either team. (Hmmmmmmm.) I wasn't picked in the second round. (Huh?) I wasn't even picked in the third round. (What?!) The hot tears I held behind my eyes made the rest of the selection process a steamy blur.

And finally, all of the picks were made.

This homerun-hero who had literally just proven her expertise and value was, again, left last. Dead last, in fact, which means that you actually were never picked; you were just the crap that was left at the end that some unlucky team has to absorb. You're the hit they have to take for the team.

This rejection made it clear to me that my peers would rather refuse to align with me than have a better chance of winning the game. I was stunned at the depth of their disdain for me, and it hurt my tender heart deeply.

I wish I knew then what I know now: There was nothing I could do to be accepted by them, and they were never going to recognize my expertise. In fact, they would even write a false narrative – that the blonde boy who struck out every time was better than me at kickball – in order to strip me of my expertise and remind me of my unworthiness. Only in retrospect can I see that the same racial bias that shaped their views and behaviors kept them from acknowledging my expertise.

By reflecting on my lived experiences with the clarity of hindsight and armed with a better understanding of how bias works, I was able to recognize that who is deemed an "expert" is very much connected to who has power, privilege, and a platform. Oppression sustains itself in part through whom we label as experts and whom we don't. The system protects itself, so those on the margins often have to actively proclaim their expertise and demand that their worth be recognized in order to claim the success they have earned.

Emboldened by that realization and recognizing that I had to stop waiting and instead try a new approach, I very matter-of-factly and unapologetically clicked "post" on my comment recommending myself on that LinkedIn call for speakers. I knew that my name belonged there. I did not know how it would land or whether it would pay off, but I knew that *not* speaking my own name would be a lie by omission, as I met all the qualifications needed to be a great candidate for this opportunity. I also thought about my responsibility to reconstruct norms to create space for *all* of us, especially for those who are most harshly judged for standing in their value: women of color. In order to reconstruct norms, we must courageously speak the truth about our expertise and not lie to make ourselves appear small, come what may.

As it turns out, the person who posted the call for speakers was intrigued by my comment to her post, checked out my work, and reached out to me soon afterwards to invite me to speak at the conference! She later shared with me that she had been impressed and inspired by my self-advocacy. It mattered to her and moved her in a meaningful way. By recommending myself, I took a chance on me, and by selecting me, she took a chance on me.

In the end, the chance we both took paid off. That speaking engagement (unironically titled, "Owning Your Value") ended up being one of the conference's most popular sessions and led to a lot of new business for me. It allowed me to broaden my impact by reaching new audiences, but it also allowed me to deepen my impact by having walked the walk in owning my own value to secure that opportunity. I can't believe how easily I could have missed out on all that just by not typing my own name.

Unfortunately, my horrible kickball experience from my youth has stayed with me both in memory and in feeling, representing a battle with society's biases that persists today. But fortunately, today, I am able to catalyze my memory and feeling into action. And that action has been to recognize why society holds certain people in certain levels of regard, and to make judgments for myself on who is an "expert" or "qualified." This shift has meant not waiting for my name to be spoken and the label "expert" bestowed upon me, but speaking my own name and claiming my own expertise.

It has meant picking myself.

NEHA SAMPAT, Esq. is CEO and founder of GenLead|BelongLab, where she focuses on building belonging and true inclusion. Through consulting, training, speaking, and writing, she helps organizations create peak-performance, inclusive teams by addressing hidden barriers to belonging, such as Imposter Syndrome and internalized bias, unconscious bias, distrust in teams, and wellness challenges. She is a nationally sought-after expert on inclusive leadership and disrupting Imposter Syndrome, and she runs the top-rated "Owning Your Value" programs to cultivate evidence-based confidence and nurture authenticity.

In her work, Neha leverages her experience working as an attorney at both large and boutique law firms, her tenure as dean of students and leadership professor, and the joys and struggles of "mama"ing her eight-year-old and seven-year-old kids. Neha's insights have been featured in *Time Magazine, Thrive Global, ABA Journal, Attorney at Work,* the *Mom Life and Law* podcast, *Dreammakers* podcast, the *Women's Advocate* podcast, and numerous other professional publications and media.

Neha holds BAs in Sociology and Political Science from University of Illinois at Urbana-Champaign, obtained her JD from UC Berkeley School of Law, received her Certificate in Graduate Applied Psychology, and is certified in Hogan personality assessment systems. Neha works across industry, from Amazon to Pixar, and UC Berkeley to Leadership Council on Legal Diversity. You can read more of Neha's insights at www.genlead.co and follow her on LinkedIn at www.linkedin.com/in/nsampat and on TW/IG/FB at @belonglab.

INTENTIONAL MINDSET: STRATEGIES AND TACTICS FOR SHIFTING MINDSET AND MOVING FORWARD

by Monica Phillips

There is one thing we can all be certain of: change is inevitable (except when it's not). So what happens when nothing seems to change?

During the pandemic, it felt like everything was stuck in place. Every day felt like Groundhog Day. Sure, some things changed...the world changed! But once it did, it all just stood still.

As someone who grew up with adversity as my middle name, I knew what I would do. I would pivot. I would practice gratitude. I would reach out to my network and pay attention to my biggest priorities. I would set great habits around eating, exercise, and sleep.

And then, I found myself exhausted. Everything felt different; I felt stuck. From Zoom fatigue to change fatigue, everything was piling on to my feelings of burnout.

Covid changed my plan to launch a six-city tour of The Legal Academy. While I quickly pivoted to online webinars, it wasn't the same. Like many, I found engaging in webinar after webinar extremely overwhelming, but I tried to focus on my value of holding space for conversations that mattered. I wanted to address the fear and anxiety we were all feeling, lean into my mission, and share my work as much as I could.

I believe that when we show up and do the work we are meant to do, people will find a way to compensate us. And that's what happened.

Two people from the webinar series hired me for wellness keynotes, and another two hired me for workshops and coaching. By showing up and doing the work I love, I was able to stay top-of-mind with those for whom my message resonated, while planting seeds for others who may have been new to the topic. Our changing world gave me time to pause and relaunch the group coaching programs that I had been wanting to get back to doing, as well.

As humans, we often have a hard time being with ourselves. As the great yogi Jeanne Heileman says, "I survived... myself."

It's difficult to sit with our busy and complex minds. To add to that, many of us suffer from things others cannot see: depression, anxiety, stress, a toxic workplace culture, fear of failure, imposter syndrome, and countless other silent battles. These mindsets are very real, and quite pervasive. Coupled with the isolation of quarantine, coming face-to-face with ourselves can feel daunting.

Change is not just about what is going on around us, but what is brewing inside of us. I needed time to rest so I would have the strength and rejuvenation to start again.

TAKE THE FIRST STEP

Have you ever started a workout when you really didn't feel like exercising? In order to get yourself to the studio, you start with just the first step: putting on the right clothes and shoes. Once you are there, you start with one move, and then one minute, and so on. You just keep going. Maybe you promised a friend you'd do a class with her, or you reserved a time for yourself at the studio. Regardless of the specifics, taking the first step can get you moving, even when you really don't feel like it.

By the time you get to the end of your workout, chances are you'll be glad you did it. Maybe you'll even wish you could do more! Other things in your day become that much better, because you already showed yourself that you could do something challenging, show up for yourself, and finish it.

How could this step-by-step practice help you move forward with work priorities or other items you've been avoiding?

BE PRESENT

As parents, we often reminisce on our child's younger days. We reflect on moments of sweetness – maybe a moment they said a word in a particularly sweet way, or that time they stopped to notice a ladybug. Those moments go by so fast. One day our kid is carrying their tiny umbrella, and the next day they are in high school.

The practice of being present is an incredible gift, allowing us to connect to the now, and the power of choice. When I feel frustrated by what isn't working, I recenter myself on the present and realize there is always something to enjoy. This positive mindset allows everything to feel a bit brighter.

"There's a sunrise and sunset every day. You can choose to be there for it. You can put yourself in the way of beauty." – Cheryl Strayed

A friend reminded me of this quote, and I love what it brings up. We can let life pass us by or we can choose to be present for it.

ALLOW YOURSELF TO BE MESSY

The first time I started a business, I allowed the process to be messy. I jumped in without always knowing what I was doing. I wasn't always aware of the mistakes I was making, so I wasn't afraid to make them. This time was different. With past experience in mind, I knew where things could go wrong. As a result, I was much more aware of what I did and didn't want to do, and more afraid to fail. The downfall? When we hold ourselves back, we block further learning experiences. We don't allow ourselves to experiment, which leaves us with nothing ventured or gained.

I wanted to continue on my growth trajectory, and this meant letting go of my newfound fear. Instead, I chose to embrace imperfection, allowing myself to be messy while experimenting with new opportunities.

LESS IS MORE

When we are intentional and focused, our opportunities expand. Contrarily, if we aren't discerning and deliberate, we lose clarity. Focus allows us to more effectively track our progress and measure our outcomes.

Have you ever tried to do it all, only to find yourself burned out or harming relationships along the way? You are not alone. I once worked at a law firm in which our team was spread extremely thin. I felt like I couldn't do anything right. When I finally had the courage to prioritize three key initiatives and postpone other work for a short period, I gained influence and people liked me more. The entire team was able to thrive by focusing on what mattered most. I continue to practice this lesson and know that when I am focused on just one or two projects, the outcomes are so much better for everyone involved.

EMBRACE AN INTEGRATED MINDSET

Sometimes we do something so many times that we begin to think that any other way of doing it would be wrong. Think about the last time you told someone "that's not how it's done," even though there may have been an alternative approach you never thought to consider. I see this in the workplace. I have often heard, "That won't work. We've tried it before."

But what would happen if you could try a task again as if you were doing it for the first time, while bringing together your entire team's depth of knowledge and experience?

I work hard to make sure my network is diverse, as this allows me to see the world through so many unique perspectives. I love to ask someone who has never tried something how they might approach it, so I can learn and grow with them.

I also love gaining new insights and wisdom from someone who has done something a thousand times, and connecting those insights with my own experiences. This integrated mindset pairs the advantage of knowledge and experience with the opportunity for continued learning and growth.

GO FOR IT

People are not always mind readers. Most of the time you have to tell them what you want and ask how they can help. This concept reminds me of Brené Brown's story of woman and shame, and how after she wrote her first book, she waited for people to read it and review it. She was afraid to tell people that she had just published a book. We can't expect someone to know what we are doing or how we need help if we don't share it with them.

I had waited five months to relaunch my group coaching program. I was overthinking it and afraid of imperfection or that no one would sign up. I finally had the courage to post it on my website. Someone in Austria saw it and signed up! I then shared the information with a friend, who proceeded to add one of her team members to the group. From there, a friend who was thinking about me reached out and asked about coaching for her team, and then invited a friend to join her. Another person saw my email newsletter and had been wanting to try this program, so she jumped in. Within five days, I had a group ready for coaching, and yet it took me five months to decide to go for it. I had to trust in myself, knowing that I had been doing the hard work, planting the right seeds, and building my community. I just had to take the next step and share it with my friends, fans, and allies. When I finally did, they were ready to be part of it.

EMBRACE ROUTINE

Excellence is a habit and that is what I practice. My routine is no exception. I wake up, drink water, practice yoga. At night, I prioritize sleep so I can wake up feeling good.

As I write this, my son has returned to in-person school two days per week, and I am feeling an enormous sense of possibility as I reclaim a routine that inspires me. In the peak of Covid, I was a bit lazier than I'd like to be. While some days I appreciated less action, I grew tired of it overall.

It feels so good to have a routine that includes habits that help shape who I am and the type of person I want to be. What habits do you want to add back into your schedule to create the excellence you envision for yourself?

CUT YOUR LOSSES

In 2004, I heard Donna Dubinsky share her top ten leadership lessons from her time as CEO of Handspring.

She had just signed a significant office space lease when sales plummeted. She had to save what she could even though it meant taking a huge loss.

Sometimes we invest so much in one idea that we are afraid to leave it. Many of us, myself included, were pushed to readjust when Covid hit. I had spent five months creating something that could not continue. The world had shut down. It was hard to let it go.

What helped me through? Remembering my 'why.' I focused on my purpose and passion for equity and inclusion in the legal industry. That's what helped me continue with next steps.

CELEBRATE YOURSELF

Throw yourself a dance party. Eat cake. Celebrate. When I cross something off my list, I have a mini dance party. But you don't have to wait until something big has been achieved to throw on some music and move around; sometimes I dance just to give myself a break and start fresh. Embrace the moment and be proud of yourself. Don't get stuck waiting to be happy. Decide to be happy now. Make this moment count.

As the founder of the Legal Academy on Equity and Inclusion and with over 20 years of experience leading teams for some of the largest law firms, **MONICA PHILLIPS** supports leaders at all levels to create thriving and inclusive workplaces through elevating leadership, mindfulness, and emotional well-being.

For the past eight years, Monica has been coaching and partnering with lawyers, startup founders, executives, and their teams in Fortune 100 companies and private organizations, including some of the best companies to work for in the U.S.

Known for her global perspective and her innovative strategies, she is a fierce advocate and proponent for inclusivity and well-being, supporting her clients to reach higher levels of health and performance.

She has a master's degree in International Education and is a Certified Professional Co- Active Coach with the leading coach organization, the Co-Active Training Institute. She is credentialed as a Professional Certified Coach with the International Coaching Federation, is a Certified Positive Intelligence Coach, and is certified in DEI in the Workplace, as an InPowered Leadership Coach, and is a 500-hour (RYT) certified yoga teacher.

You can find her online at www.sparkpluglabs.co.

THE PROCESS OF DECISION-MAKING

by Donald Snead

The topic of decision-making, in and of itself, is an interesting one. There are many ways in which a person can engage this process. The decision-making process for complex, life changing decisions – which often affect one's personal life and/or career – is even more challenging. Now, let's throw in the fact that I'm a lawyer who specializes in helping other lawyers navigate their next job pursuit; it should make for a fun chapter.

Lawyers, by nature, are all about getting the facts, leaving out the feelings, and persuading others toward a specific conclusion. With that said, you would think that coming to a decision (for a lawyer) would be an overtly simplified process. Sadly, that's not the case. You see, this simple process is complicated by its very simplicity. Since every major career decision is ripe with important factors to consider, a lawyer's way of thinking typically forces them to overanalyze and scrutinize each and every element that plays into a decision. This, not surprisingly, makes the relatively simple process of decision-making far more complex than it should be.

I've spent the last several years of my career working as an executive recruiter, simultaneously helping companies identify and address gaps within their upper echelons of their workforce and working with attorneys (and other executives) to find their next, great career opportunity. In short, a big part of my job is to present people with career options that can significantly affect their professional and personal life for several years to come. Some are at greater ease than others when it comes to either accepting or declining a position, and I've often wondered if I have ever made the decision appealing enough or more difficult to make. Regardless, my process of decision-making – which I often share with candidates – has always been the same. I take into consideration the company's, as well as the candidate's, strongest values and ensure that they align even before I present an opportunity. This typically levels out the playing field for all of us. Not to mention, it usually places the right candidate in the best place.

Now, most decisions presented to us are almost never presented quite *that* neatly. They often come at us out of nowhere and usually come at a cost. How do you navigate through your decision-making process? Do you go at it alone? Do you have a specific number of opinions that you need to hear prior to you coming up with your own? Does it make you feel like crawling into a ball and waiting for the decision to simply pass over you? Or are you the "go with your gut" kind of decision maker?

As I mentioned in the beginning of this chapter, there are many different ways one can go about their decision-making process. Let's go over the typical steps someone would take to make a decision.

- Identify the decision
- Consider the opportunity
- Consider the options or the alternatives
- Ask others for their trusted opinions
- Evaluate
- Decide

Sounds simple enough, right?

Well, let me be candid so you can see a lawyer's decision-making process in real time. I had to navigate through a decision that involved my career as well as my personal life. The decision was to either pursue becoming a partner or be a present father. Sadly, my life's circumstances, at that time, would not allow me to attain both. Assessing my situation and making the correct decision for myself and my family was extremely difficult since I could make a successful case for choosing either option.

This would be a first for me. Decision-making typically came easily. First of all, I knew that I wanted to become a lawyer at the age of ten. From there, I became focused on taking the necessary steps to become one: obtain great grades, strive to place at the top of my class consistently, and play an active role in the necessary clubs and organizations. If I simply followed those steps, the outcome was inevitable. Of course, as I got older, the decisions became harder. My simple plan also neglected to address any potential variables, especially ones that I could not control.

Now, let's go over the typical steps of decision-making again, except this time, we're going to keep my decision in mind.

- I was given a choice: my personal advancement or my family's stability and success.
- I obviously could not choose whether I wanted to work or if I wanted to be a father since both were non-negotiable.
- I was, however, faced with the tough question of how I wanted to work to succeed in both areas of my life.
- I asked those whose opinions I valued.
- I weighed out each scenario and calculated each potential consequence. If I chose to pursue a successful career, I would be able to provide for my family – possibly even raise my daughter to have everything she needed or wanted without a financial strain. Although, would that come at a cost? Would I be around to enjoy the life that I had provided and worked so hard to obtain alongside my family? Or would I be buried in work and obligations? On the other hand, if I chose to truly be a present father and actively raise my daughter, would I regret the lack of career advancement into which I had poured my entire life? There were so many things to take into consideration.
- Then I made a decision.

As a lawyer, you learn to tame your feelings. If you're a practicing litigator, you're trained to never lose your cool. Remain unflappable. "You're emotionless." "You're cold." "You're despondent." I've heard these terms almost my entire adult life. Truth be told, I can see why people say this, though it's not accurate. I'm merely constantly thinking – weighing out the pros and cons of every scenario, making decisions every step of the way. Critical thinking and being deep in thought have always been a part of my process, so it makes me seem distant.

This process, although thorough and most times helpful, has also impacted my ability to allow others in on the process. A lot of times, one's decisions do not only affect themselves. Even indirectly, the ripple effect of your decision will eventually dictate or influence someone else's decision-making process.

According to a survey by Columbia University published in *Psychology Today,* the average American makes approximately seventy conscious decisions each and every day. So approximately seventy times every day, you and I try to make sense of our own very complicated world. Deciding whether to focus on this or that, turn left or right, go up or down, choose career or family. Their worth or my self-worth? Honestly, it's draining.

There's so much pressure in trying to make the right decision, especially when it will directly affect more than just yourself. So why not remove that pressure? Instead of weighing yourself down with the idea of having to choose between Option A and Option B, do your research, go through your process, then simply commit. I know; easier said than done, but let me explain.

When we have a choice in front of us, it seems easier to muddy the waters and pressure ourselves into the thought of potentially making the wrong decision rather than walking ourselves through an objective process. Therefore, we easily get stuck in the decision itself. We have to remind ourselves that since there are so many factors that are out of our control, all we can do is gather the facts that we are certain of and compare those options.

Once we've made the decision, we have to allow ourselves the room to celebrate making that decision and commit to growing into that decision. Set yourself up for success in your new scenario. Once that decision and situation has run its course, you will be presented with a new one. Regardless of how successful or unsuccessful the decision, you can be proud of being committed to your decision and giving it your best effort.

People will often remind you to learn how to overcome certain challenges. I urge you to learn the art of "how" to make a decision wisely. Something I learned early on in life in regard to making decisions is that success does not come from being able to make the decision itself, but from making the decision and carrying that decision through with 100% commitment.

I did it! I made my decision to be a present and active father in my daughter's life. Once I came to that decision, I committed and never looked back. Call it lucky or a blessing, but the universe kindly confirmed my decision by letting me live fully alongside my family and do meaningful work in something that I committed to long before I had any decisions to make.

Being an attorney, then and now, meant that I could help someone in need. The decisions I've made along the way may have contributed to my career looking a lot different than what I had originally imagined, but it has been the best decision that I have ever made. My decision-making process will certainly be very different from yours, but once you figure out what your process looks like and you learn to commit to your decisions, I'm sure that your success will be right around the corner.

DONALD A. SNEAD, a lawyer by training, is an executive recruiter with Spencer Stuart in Chicago. He has broad finance, legal, education and non-profit executive search experience across all industries. Prior to joining Spencer Stuart in 2019, Donald practiced law at Orrick, Herrington & Sutcliffe LLP and Perkins Coie LLP, and he was an early member of FLEX by Fenwick, Fenwick & West LLP's legal consulting arm, all in the San Francisco Bay Area.

Donald earned his J.D. from the Northwestern University Pritzker School of Law, his Ed.M. from the Harvard University Graduate School of Education, graduating cum laude, and his B.A. in Individualized Study from New York University, graduating magna cum laude.

THE 'ME-FIRST' MINDSET

by Amy Friederich

Me-First Mindset: A mindset approach to overcoming workplace burnout and increasing occupational well-being.

You probably heard the phrases "self-care" and "work-life balance" more in the year 2020 than in your entire life. The COVID-19 pandemic flipped our daily routines upside down, forcing us to examine what our lives had become and where they were headed. For many, this was especially true within our careers, as we tried to balance our work lives with our home lives.

About six weeks into the stay-at-home order, I was laid off from my cushy corporate legal recruiting position. After a few tears and minor freak-outs, I felt relieved. I had been unhappy in my position since the company relocated to an area that tripled my commute. Prior to the pandemic, I had asked my boss if I could work from home a few days per week, and she told me that was impossible. Of course, once the stay-at-home orders were in place, we seamlessly transitioned to remote work. Go figure!

I was mostly relieved about losing my job, because I suddenly had the time and motivation to pursue a professional goal of mine: starting a yoga business. I had been teaching yoga part-time for about four years, and had an idea to create a business where I could work with busy professionals one-on-one in their homes and offices. I wanted to offer a convenient service that was customized to their needs and fit their schedules. So, I did. I dove right in and founded Amy Lynn Yoga. Since then, I have been working with individual clients, as well as with groups, bringing yoga and other wellness programs into clients' homes and offices. While I first only offered these services virtually, I am gradually adding in-person options to the mix.

The motivation for my business came from my experience as a former trial lawyer. I started working within big law right out of law school, practicing civil defense litigation. Four years into my law practice, I felt extremely burned out, as my firm pressured me to increase my monthly billable hours. I began coming into the office on the weekends, and everyone in my social circle was also a lawyer. I needed an outlet.

Motivated to meet new people, study a subject that was new and interesting to me, and learn more about the practice, I enrolled in yoga teacher training. I never intended to teach yoga, but once I got started, I was hooked. I started out by teaching once a week at a yoga studio, as well as pop-up events around the city a few times a month. It was my 'fun job' and exactly the outlet I needed from my legal career. I learned so much about myself and how to live my life with purpose, gratitude, and compassion.

I also learned that it was okay, and in fact necessary, to put myself first. I realized that putting myself first did not make me selfish or self-centered. After all, what good am I to others if I am not okay? As a lawyer, I was always handling other peoples' problems and trying to please my partners and clients. I began to understand that I needed to cultivate a sense of balance.

During my yoga teacher training, I realized that I did not want to work within the traditional law firm culture for the rest of my career, given the demanding workload and stressful environment. So, I took a legal recruiter position, allowing me more of a nine-to-five schedule, increased PTO, and the opportunity to work with a diverse group of young professionals. Despite my gripe about the longer commute that later followed, I really did enjoy that role.

However, the transition from private practice to a non-traditional legal role was not easy. I often received judgmental looks and condescending remarks about not practicing law. These comments came from other lawyers, my own family and friends, and even total strangers. As you can imagine, I've received even more now that I teach yoga full-time. Regardless, it was imperative to create a career that aligned with my desired lifestyle and core values.

To accomplish this, I had to do a lot of self-reflection. I wrote down my priorities in life, my passions, my skills, and the type of lifestyle I wanted. I also had to thoroughly examine my financial situation. I even met with a career counselor for several sessions, something I still do on occasion and highly recommend to anyone struggling with career satisfaction.

I have since found a way to combine my years of experience working in the legal field with my yoga teaching business. Afterall, I would have never pursued yoga teacher training if it were not for the challenges I faced as a practicing attorney. My journey led me to my mission: to motivate legal professionals to prioritize their physical, mental, and occupational well-being, whether that is through yoga or some other form of self-care that better serves them.

I've put this mission into action in many ways. I created a continuing legal education (CLE) program called Self-Care for Legal Professionals that has been approved for 1.2 hours of CLE credit. In addition, I have led virtual yoga and meditation sessions for various law firms and legal organizations, including the Women Lawyers Association, The American Bar Association Young Lawyers Division, and The Bar Association of Metropolitan St. Louis (BAMSL).

Through Amy Lynn Yoga, I hope to inspire women, lawyers, and others within high-stress positions to demand what they need for a better work-life balance (or work-life blend as many now call it) and to make time for self-care. I am not suggesting that burned out lawyers quit the legal field or give up their practice. We need to keep good lawyers, especially women (who left the workforce at higher rates than men during the pandemic to care for loved ones),

160

in the profession. But for many women, returning to the workforce post-pandemic will require increased flexibility, such as remote work options or flexible hours.

One of the topics I touch on in the Self-Care for Legal Professionals program involves finding a passion outside of the legal field (or in whichever industry you might work). Being a lawyer, for example, is not the type of job you can clock in and out of. (Even now, people still ask me for legal advice or opinions on a trending legal issue or new court ruling!) It is so easy to identify ourselves with what we do for a living. Thus, it is important to have interests and hobbies unrelated to work. For me, it was yoga, music, and travel. For others, it could be gardening, cycling, or volunteering for an animal rescue. Regardless, having an outlet outside of work allows us to better connect with ourselves physically, mentally, and spiritually.

Practicing self-care on a regular basis, even when it is more trivial, is also key. Whether it's getting a pedicure, taking a bath, or cooking, self-care results in greater balance, and more happiness.

Self-care requires a 'me-first' mindset because it must be incorporated into our hectic schedules and treated like any other appointment or commitment. It also requires compassion and gentleness towards oneself. When we are kind to ourselves, we are more likely to be compassionate and empathetic to others.

But compassion towards others must be paired with honoring our own personal boundaries.

Learning to say "no" has always been a struggle for me. To this day, I feel guilty if someone asks me for something and I am unable to help them out, or wants to spend time with me when I am unavailable. However, I am learning that it is okay to say no. Recently, I have even started learning to say no without giving a reason for it. This is tough, as it is natural (or perhaps habitual) to want to explain myself to other people, but I'm realizing that I really do not owe anyone an explanation. In most instances, no one seems offended or upset, or even asks me to explain. I have found people to be more understanding than anticipated.

We live in a world where many people measure success and self-worth by how much money they make, rather than by how happy they are. I still find myself explaining to people why I chose yoga over law, and it is so hard to let go of what other people think. But I constantly remind myself of my "why" in these instances: my yoga and meditation practice help me stay focused on my personal and professional goals.

I admit I do not practice every day, and some days I still struggle with occupational well-being, especially when it comes to reconciling my identity as a lawyer with that of a yoga teacher. However, I have learned that I do not have to have everything perfectly figured out. Life is a continuous journey of self-discovery and growth. So long as I have a 'me-first' mindset and remain full of love and compassion, I know I am on the right track.

AMY FRIEDERICH is a licensed attorney and certified yoga teacher based in St. Louis, Missouri. She has worked in the legal field for over fifteen years in a variety of roles, having worked her way up from receptionist to attorney. In addition to law, Amy has a passion for teaching. She has been teaching yoga since 2016 and teaching Business Law at Lewis and Clark Community College since 2018.

Her blended expertise provides her the ability to personally relate to other lawyers, educators, and professionals who may be struggling to prioritize their well-being and find work-life balance. That is why she created Amy Lynn Yoga, LLC, a yoga and wellness company catering specifically to professionals. She offers private yoga instruction to individual clients as well as group classes for businesses who understand the benefits of having an employee wellness program. She has also worked with professional organizations, like The Woman Lawyers Association and The American Bar Association, as well as nonprofits, to raise awareness and normalize conversations around the importance of prioritizing self-care, including physical, mental, and occupational well-being.

When she is not teaching lawyers downward dog, Amy enjoys spending time at home with her two pit bull mixes or traveling abroad with her fiancé. For more information about her background or business, please visit www.amylynnyogastl.com.

SEEKING SUCCESS

by Christy Freer

I've spent a lifetime trying to be "that person." You know, the one who can do it all and look good doing it, who can be both smart and popular, the "it" girl who can light up a room, drive conversation, motivate teammates, achieve amazing results, and make others wonder how she does it all.

For external purposes, some would say I've done that, or at least been that person at various points throughout my career. Some people think that I've always lived a life that achieves this lofty goal, and certainly looks like that: big law job, caring husband, beautiful children, house, car, great hair, etc. But here's the secret: they've got it all wrong, and I'm a total fraud. (Or at least my Facebook and Instagram feeds don't tell the whole story of who I am and how I got here.) Does anyone else feel this way?

I've done a lot of soul-searching over the past year, and indeed over the past ten years, as I've made some major career and relationship changes in my life. What I discovered is that I was so busy pursuing the traditional (and too often, impossible) notion of success that I never really stopped to think about what I actually, truly wanted. I never entertained the idea that I might want something off the well-trodden corporate path, because the thought seemed so open-ended, so without a safety net, that it scared the heck out of me. Once I started asking myself those big questions, I realized that the answers were, of course, a combination of "I don't know what I want" and "not this." Those answers, and the quest to find them, eventually led me through divorce, a departure from big law, a yoga teacher training program and pilgrimages through India, adoption of a different faith tradition, a long stint as in-house counsel, new marriage, another child, and another career shift, with a lot of growth and development along the way. So, what was the secret? How did I figure out what I wanted, and how did I lean into getting it?

Well, there is no secret, really. Everything that I came to realize has always been there for all of us to see – I just didn't want to see it. I wanted to will it out of existence. The fact of the matter is that the cards are stacked against us, and by "us" I mean women. Women in general, but in particular working women, even more so working moms (especially during the pandemic), and even more acutely black women, LGBTQ women and any women who dare to challenge or question the system that holds us back.

It wasn't a matter of somehow pushing through all of that, beating the system, or finding the ever elusive "balance" we all talk about achieving. (I hate to be the bearer of bad news, but balance is a total myth.) For me, getting to "success" really became about turning those traditional notions upside down. I had to shift my perspective so I could see all these things differently. I had to examine what I was truly seeking, and whether it would make me happy in the end. It took me a long time to figure out what to look for instead.

I WANTED IT TO BE EASY

For some odd reason, I thought that getting to success the "normal" way would be easy. I wanted to just do my work as a big law associate and do it well and have that naturally lead to partnership and business development opportunities and a cushy life with lots of financial security and career satisfaction. I'm aware of the immense privilege that allowed that to even be a thought in my mind. After all, things had been relatively easy so far. Sure, I worked hard, but I had opportunities handed to me on a silver platter. I didn't have to beat the streets looking for my big law job. I didn't have to chase down partners for work assignments to advance my career. But something still didn't feel right. I didn't see anyone among the partners whose life really exemplified what I wanted, once you scratched beneath the surface. I didn't know anyone who didn't have to make huge sacrifices to get where they wanted to go, where I wanted to go – and those were sacrifices that, over time, I realized I didn't want to make. Still, I soldiered on, convinced that somehow, I would be different. I would be able to do what they hadn't. Things were changing, but they never really change, or at least not fast enough for me.

I had everything coming to me, but I still wasn't happy. It didn't feel like I thought it should. I couldn't enjoy my success. I had health challenges. At first I could ignore them and just push through. But when I reached a point where I ended up in the hospital for a month, I finally had to confront the fact that I was not okay. I have an autoimmune condition that affects my digestive system, my joints, my muscles and my skin. At some point, my body said 'enough is enough' and just shut down. At that time, I didn't even know how to prioritize my health, much less what to do to fix the damage I'd inflicted on my body through a decade of neglect. So, I followed a friend who suggested I join her for yoga.

Now, this is not going to be one of those love-at-first-sight, immediate breakthrough, yoga-changed-my-life kind of stories. It did, but it took time. It also took understanding a different idea of what "yoga" means. It wasn't a one stop shop; I still had to go through a lot of medical work to heal myself, work that continues to this day. I was also stubborn. I resisted. After all, this was time I was taking away from my desk billing, and my body and my brain didn't like that. But after a few classes, I figured out that when I breathed deeply during a yoga class, it felt different to me because it was the first and only time that I had taken a deep breath that whole day. Or week. Or since I last went to yoga. I thought there was something worth exploring there.

TURNS OUT, I WAS RIGHT

In addition to my health challenges, which naturally included mental wellbeing as well as physical wellbeing challenges, I had relationship issues. I was clearly with the wrong partner. Again, I sort of knew that from the beginning, but didn't stop to ask why I shouldn't marry the "it" boy, the most handsome one, the funny and charming guy, the one that all my friends wanted. Never mind that we thought differently about the world, were nowhere near the same in our levels of maturity or what we wanted in life, and had different ideas about what our future family life would be like. We never asked those questions. Neither of us bothered to learn how to be good partners, even to someone who was on the same page, much less to someone as different as we were to each other! He couldn't support me through my illness. I couldn't support him as he floundered in getting his career established. At some point, we both realized that we needed to move forward in life separately so we could do right by ourselves and our child, and thankfully parted amicably. As I look back, all the signs were there.

The amount of cognitive dissonance we all engage in to try to make the world be what we've been told that it should be, instead of what we see unfolding before us every day, is really astounding. I realized I had been doing that in my marriage, my career, and with my health. But why? Why were my expectations of reality so different than what I encountered? Why did I think I could will things into being different? What was I supposed to do with all these grand realizations?

SO, WHAT NOW?

Those are the questions I asked myself in 2012, after going through a divorce, a year of teaching yoga, a shift to an in-house job to pay the bills, and another debilitating auto-immune flare up. (No wonder, really, with that kind of stress in my life.)

In the end, I'm grateful for all the adversity that forced me to find the right questions and seek better answers. Here's the thing, though: there is no answer. There is no seven-step plan, or three things you should do every day, or exercise program, or self-care routine, or any system that if you somehow figured out, you could magically become that person who inspires wonder in everyone she meets. That person doesn't exist, because you're never seeing the full story.

There's no amount of yoga, or exercise, or meditation that will undo the patriarchy, create truly equal opportunities for women and people of color, eliminate injustice in the legal system and make the expectations of women in our society any more rational or achievable. There's nothing that we are doing wrong by not somehow having figured this out on an individual level, despite all that society tells us to the contrary.

I am never going to feel like life is fair for me or my children, and it's never going to be easy for me to achieve those traditional markers of success. But what my explorations through yoga, meditation, breathing, music and faith have taught me is that my goal, what I truly want, is something different.

I don't need to change the world, beat the system or rail against my inability to do so. What I need to do is to somehow live my life, do my best, and be ok no matter what happens. It's really that simple. I need to be able to know that some days my best might not be enough, and not let that feel like defeat. I need to observe my joys and cherish them, knowing that they will be fleeting, and that a new and different happiness awaits around the next corner.

SEEKING EQUANIMITY

My definition of success at this point in my life is seeking equanimity – the ability to move through life undisturbed by the ebb and flow of happiness and distress, and the ability to get up each day and face whatever life throws at me without letting it define me or derail me. I don't have to achieve this every day, and it changes moment by moment, but it is enough for me now to return to the practice, to understand that everything in life is temporary, and to maintain the longer-term view that a perspective grounded in equanimity can offer. It seems so small, on the one hand, and yet it is the biggest endeavor I've ever attempted.

Now, this does not mean that I move through life with less passion or energy – far from it. What it does mean is that I feel like I am spending a lot less time wasting that energy. I am not replaying or imagining scenarios in my head, wondering 'what-if', or chasing down 'opportunities' that will elevate my worth in the eyes of others but that are not in line with my values and my vision for my future. I don't suppress my emotions, but rather, pause and observe. Consequently, I am better able to respond to the demands of the moment without letting my emotions carry me to a place of negativity or non-productive action.

I have come to accept that I am not 'normal' in the traditional, corporate sense, and never will be. And to embrace my weirdness as a true asset! It means that I can work to be of service and to improve the lives of others with a certain amount of detachment from the broader results, so that I can do that work with a clear sense of hope and purpose rather than disappointment or disillusionment.

We humans are the only species on the planet that really gets to inquire about why we're here and what we want. It would be a shame to waste that unique opportunity living our lives "asleep" to those answers, feeling controlled by others' expectations, and frittering away our energy on fruitless pursuits. Maintaining the perspective that a lens of equanimity can offer is a constant work in progress, but with the right tools, it becomes a welcome exercise, and one that can create a greater sense of ease in all we do.

CONCLUSION

Everyone has their own definition of success. Acknowledging and creating space for that reality, for ourselves and others, is an achievement in and of itself. My hope for all of us is that we seek to define our own path, grant ourselves the grace to explore and develop our own tools to aid us along the way, and have the courage and fortitude to not be swayed when life tries to take us off course. "Success" is there for the taking; it is up to us how we get there.

CHRISTY FREER is a Banking & Finance counsel in Mayer Brown's Washington DC office. Christy focuses her practice on representing issuers, borrowers, underwriters and commercial banks in a wide variety of financing facilities backed by credit card receivables and auto and equipment loans and leases, in both the public and private markets. Christy has also been a leader in developing the financing of commercial property assessed clean energy (C-PACE) assets, deploying technology routinely utilized in securitizing other asset classes to help build scale in the C-PACE market. She is also part of the firm's global IBOR Transition Task Force, advising on the use of AI tools in broad-scale IBOR remediation.

Christy is widely regarded as a trusted business partner and efficient problem solver, who leverages her unique experience both as in-house counsel and in private practice to anticipate and address client needs. Outside of her legal practice, Christy is a mom, registered yoga teacher and accomplished musician who still performs locally and facilitates yoga/music educational workshops in her spare time. She also serves as a mentor to several younger attorneys, both at Mayer Brown and throughout the industry.

Prior to joining Mayer Brown, Christy was a senior director and associate general counsel at Capital One Financial Corporation, where she led the legal support for all corporate treasury activities. In her in-house role, Christy managed a diverse mix of capital markets funding platforms, including unsecured transactions and securitization programs backed by card, auto and mortgage assets and related regulatory and compliance considerations. She also covered derivatives and liability management transactions, and worked closely with her colleagues on capital markets-focused M&A as well as company disclosure and governance matters. Before joining Capital One, Christy was a senior associate in the Washington, DC office of Orrick, Herrington & Sutcliffe LLP.

HERE AND THERE MINDSET
CULTIVATING GRATITUDE WHERE YOU ARE WHILE RELENTLESSLY PURSUING WHERE YOU WANT TO BE

by David Hamm

A brief glance at my resume exposes that I have been all over the place educationally and vocationally. I received my undergraduate degree in business management, then a masters in theology, juris doctor and am currently nearly the completion of an LL.M. at Georgetown in Securities and Financial Regulation. I have made eight vocational transitions since my law school graduation in 2008, ranging from big firms, small firms, teaching law, doing both law and church work, and working in-house at a F150 company. Not exactly a model of stability.

In reflecting back on so many of those years and transitions, I have self-diagnosed myself with what I call the "grass-is-greener" or "restless soul" syndrome (RSS). There is nothing wrong with being restless, most of the interesting people in my life share that characteristic with me. However, a potential dark side of restlessness is the failure to be grateful for one's current situation. Sure, there are always things that are not good about our current situations. There are things that need to change, both within and without. But, there are always countless things that we should be thankful for even if nothing about our current situation changes.

THE LIES BENEATH RSS

There are at least three lies beneath RSS, as applied to the vocational space. These lies can manifest themselves in degrees, but the basic thrusts are:

- There is nothing good about my current job;
- Another job will finally provide the satisfaction that I have been wanting;
- My current flaws will not follow me to a new job.

One of the most powerful things about a lie is that it never delivers what it promises. As one who has made several vocational transitions, I have experienced the failure of these lies to deliver. The truth is that there is always something good about your current job, a new job will never fully provide the satisfaction that you crave and your current flaws always seem to travel with you from one job to the next.

A PROPOSED PATH FORWARD:
Rediscovering the "Here" by Cultivating Gratitude

LinkedIn has enhanced my professional life in several ways. One of the most trajectory changing moments for me was a short article about cultivating gratitude. Like most concepts that provide significant change, it wasn't complicated. The article simply suggested that the reader take one minute a day for three months and write down things that they were thankful for. I took the bait and didn't stop after the three-month suggested time period. The exercise continued for several years with thousands of reasons for gratitude being recorded in my Evernote app. It didn't take a significant amount of time, but the exercise had a significant impact on my mindset.

My father always told me that if you don't enjoy today, chances are you will not enjoy tomorrow, and then your life will pass by without you enjoying it. The discipline of cultivating gratitude helped me to stop believing the lies beneath RSS and to embrace my current role with a spirit of gratitude. Some days were (and are) better than others. Like any practice, cultivating gratitude takes practice. Given my natural tendencies, I lean towards noticing what is wrong with my current role rather than being grateful for the many positive aspects of my current role. I naturally tend to believe that another role would magically make me happy and downsize my faults and weaknesses.

Cultivating gratitude helps me swim against the current of my natural tendencies and to embrace a spirit of gratitude. I've observed that it is very hard to grumble and be grateful at the same time. The path of gratitude casts everything about your current role in a new light. Problem people and issues remain, but a spirit of gratitude helps you assume positive intent, forgive and move on rather than festering in unforgiveness and replaying wrongs over and over again, and engage fully with others and tasks in ways that seek solutions from a broader perspective. It also allows you to embrace the "now" or the "here" of your vocational journey. You can be present where you are, with all that you are.

REDISCOVERING THE "THERE" THROUGH RELENTLESS PURSUIT

So, now we should just be grateful in the "here" and forget goals, planning, growth and pursuit of the "there," right? While I do see some people end in that spot, I don't think that is the best path. One of the greatest discoveries that I have made over these past several years is that cultivating gratitude in the here/now is the best place from which to relentlessly pursue whatever your "there" looks like. In fact, it wasn't until I started cultivating gratitude that I was able to put pen to paper on my vocational goals that I track to this day.

While it will look a bit different for everyone, I used my Evernote app to write down what I wanted the balance of my vocational years to look like. My list, crafted in 2018, includes thirteen items. Some of the items are related to educational pursuits (e.g., receiving my LL.M. from Georgetown), some of the items are related to direct vocational pursuits (e.g., becoming a GC/CLO of a public company) and some of the items are related to what I think of as indirect vocational pursuits (e.g., publishing papers in my areas of practice on a certain cadence). Each of the items has a projected time horizon and relates to the other items in some way.

I evaluate the items on my "there" list on a regular cadence and make changes as I gain a better understanding of what I want my "there" to look like or the underlying facts. For example, given that my ultimate vocational goal is to become a GC/CLO of a public company, I am always exploring different paths that could get me to that desired "there." My current role is not a direct GC-report role and, in my current thinking, the next logical step in my relentless pursuit of "there" would be landing a direct GC-report role. While that could possibly occur at my current company, it is very unlikely given the size of the legal department and relative tenure considerations. As a result, I will most likely have to move out to move up. That leads me to be on the constant lookout for roles that fit that description, cultivating relationships with legal recruiters, engagement with various organizations that could help facilitate that goal, etc. In other words, relentless pursuit despite setbacks, numerous rejection emails and dead ends. Again, wisdom from my father regarding dating back in high school applies to my job search – He always said that it only takes one yes and that the worst that the others can do is say no and that really isn't all that bad.

PUTTING IT ALL TOGETHER

It is easy to get lost in the relentless pursuit of "there." However, the great grounder is cultivating contentment in the "here." And, that is the power of the here and there mindset – *cultivating gratitude where you are (here) while relentlessly pursuing where you want to be (there).* It is a daily journey where I err on both extremes – embracing here to the exclusion of the relentless pursuit of there or relentlessly pursuing there without cultivating gratitude in the here.

Many have written/talked about the urgent drowning out the important and the need to push against that current. Three practices that can help fight that trend and move towards an adoption of the here and there mindset are:

- *Gratitude Journal* – If you have never tried a gratitude journal, I can't recommend it highly enough. I would recommend getting an app on your phone like Evernote so that you can do it at any time and in any place. A good start would be to take one minute a day for a month and list things that you are grateful for. It is okay if you repeat things day over day. The point is to prime the gratitude pump. I think you will see that the practice begins to spread beyond that one-minute window!

- *There Journal* – If you have never taken the time to write out what you would want the balance of your vocational journey to look like, give it a try. Again, I would recommend using an app like Evernote so you can have it with you at all times and make tweaks as the inspiration hits. Put a timeline for each item (it can move as many times as you want, but you should start somewhere) and think through how the items relate to each other.

- *Regular Check Ins/Actions* – Once you have your there journal in place, I recommend reviewing at a regular cadence so that you can tweak as you gain a better understanding of yourself or what you want your there to look like. I also recommend taking daily practical steps toward the fulfillment of the items outlined in your there journal. For example, I have two job searches in LinkedIn that I look at daily. It takes less than thirty seconds, but it allows me to see all the new jobs posted on LinkedIn that are within the next step on my there journal and leads to many good discussions and network building.

Like any mindset, the here and there mindset is a daily journey. Grace is needed. Starts and restarts are required. Perfection needs to be abandoned. But, as one of my wise uncles always said, we have time for what we make time for. I would encourage you to make time to cultivate gratitude as you relentlessly pursue your vocational goals. It has been a great help to me in my journey and I hope it helps you in yours.

DAVID HAMM is Senior Counsel – Corporate at Summit Materials where he provides legal support for the company's board and its committees, SEC filings and other disclosure matters, mergers and acquisitions and commercial transactions.

He graduated from the Paul M. Hebert Law Center, Louisiana State University in 2008 and is currently pursuing an LL.M. from Georgetown University Law Center in Financial Regulation and Securities (projected graduation December 2021).

David is co-chair of the In-House Subcommittee of the ABA Corporate Governance Committee and, in connection with the subcommittee's activities, is currently recording an upcoming ABA podcast entitled *Conversations with GCs* designed to educate and develop aspiring general counsels by interviewing leading general counsels for the purpose of exploring the path that led them to becoming a general counsel, essential skills and characteristics of a successful general counsel, current issues that are of a particular focus for general counsel and advice for aspiring general counsels. He and his family are based in the Denver area and try to find as much time as possible to hike, ski and explore.

This book is not a book by licensed therapists or counselors. Sharing personal stories is not a substitute for counseling, psychotherapy or any mental health services. Nothing in this book should be considered therapy or therapeutic advice or counseling.